Praise for *The Four Elements o*

"Right there in the name—*Elements of the Wise*—Ivo Dominguez Jr. reveals a key and his willingness to share his knowledge. In a day when the Elements are frequently mistaken for their tools, he opens the door to the deeper mystery and magic, encouraging a relationship with these primal powers, rooted in his vast experience, deep reflection, and practical working as a modern witch. Ivo generously shares teachings from the Assembly of the Sacred Wheel and encourages us to look at things in a different light, while remaining firmly grounded in the traditions that have come before. I've benefited from his elemental workshops, which always impress upon me a new way to look at things. I'm really filled with joy to see these teachings, in the form of this book, make their way to a larger audience that will benefit from them as much as I have."

—Christopher Penczak, award-winning author of the Temple of Witchcraft series, *Spirit Allies,* and *The Mighty Dead*

"In the *Four Elements of the Wise,* Ivo Dominguez Jr. brings exquisite depth to a topic that too many magical practitioners unfortunately take for granted. His exploration of the Elements is exceptional and profound, providing fantastic insight into an often-overlooked area. Ever graceful and thorough in presentation, Ivo helps the reader build multifaceted connections to the elemental powers. Revelations abound that will truly deepen ritual technique for new and experienced folks alike."

—Laura Tempest Zakroff, author of *Sigil Witchery* and *Weave the Liminal*

"Most books on the subject of the elements provide only a superficial understanding of these forces that are a cornerstone of magick. Ivo Dominguez Jr., a modern master of the magickal mystery traditions, remedies this in his brilliant and much needed book, *The Four*

Elements of the Wise. If you seek to deepen your relationship with the elements beyond introductory level books, connect with the elemental spirits, tune into the sub-elements of each element, and have a nuanced understanding of the subtle differences of the fifth elements of Ether, Spirit, Quintessence, then this book will greatly enhance your mastery of these universal energies."

—Mat Auryn, author of *Psychic Witch*

THE
Four
Elements
of the Wise

THE
Four
Elements
of the Wise

Working with the Magickal Powers of
Earth, Air, Water, Fire

IVO DOMINGUEZ JR.

foreword by Courtney Weber

Weiser Books

This edition first published in 2021 by Weiser Books, an imprint of
Red Wheel/Weiser, LLC
With offices at:
65 Parker Street, Suite 7
Newburyport, MA 01950
www.redwheelweiser.com

ISBN: 978-1-57863-710-2
Library of Congress Cataloging-in-Publication Data available upon request.

Cover design by Kasandra Cook
Interior images by Ivo Dominguez Jr.
Interior by Kasandra Cook
Typeset in Berkeley

Printed in the United States of America
IBI
10 9 8 7 6 5 4 3 2 1

This book is dedicated to my beloved James Conrad Welch,
and to all my community in the Assembly of the Sacred Wheel.

Contents

Acknowledgements

A special thanks to Aeptha, T. Thorn Coyle, James E. Dickinson, Katrina Messenger, and Michael G. Smith for many long conversations. I also give honor and merit to Dolores Ashcroft-Nowicki and Shakmah Winddrum for what I have learned in their presence.

Foreword

Our simplest moments are often our most profound. Or maybe our most profound moments are surprisingly simple. Either way, my first conversation with Ivo Dominguez, Jr., was a mere five minutes on a warm summer day in Connecticut. Ivo offered a kind word. I was too rattled from a stressful ritual experience to understand that I had just met someone who would change my life in many profound ways. In that brief gem of a moment, I met the man who not only introduced me to my husband but who also became my invaluable mentor.

Like many other witches, the early days of my witchcraft journey were exhilarating. No longer constrained by the dogmatic religious traditions of my youth, I relished a doctrine in which "doing what feels right" was the main code. But after a few years on this liberating path, that model offered its own constraints. If all I am to do is follow what feels right, am I just imagining my experiences? Are we all just making it up as we go along? What does a witch do when magick hurls chaos into an already chaotic existence? What happens if "doing what feels right" leads to casting spells that don't work at all? This is when many people abandon witchcraft, believing it to be pointless. Some witches, like me, are stubborn enough to stick around. They begin to seek structure.

These are the witches who need Ivo Dominguez, Jr.

It is an honor to write this foreword. For over a decade, Ivo has been the person I go to with my toughest magickal challenges. Whether it's the right oil blend, the strongest circle casting, or the management of the toughest group, Ivo has never shied away from taking the time to thoroughly, but gently, explain every answer. This experience is not unique to me. His perpetual patience and willingness to share his incredible expanse of knowledge is truly remarkable.

When I first experienced Ivo's work, I was relieved. Finally, an application of witchcraft that made sense. His approach was based on reason, trial, and error. Intuition had a role but no longer bore the pressure of being the barometer of effective magick. Ivo embodied, to me, both scientist and occultist; someone who could articulate the mechanics of magick to a witch of any level of experience, helping the newest ones to understand and the most experienced to expand their knowledge base. His demeanor was not one of "he knows better" but that of someone who has dedicated his life to the craft, motivated by pure passion for it. There is a genuine kindness to Ivo's approach, the reflection of someone who truly wants people to make effective magick and lead productive, fulfilling lives as a result.

Ivo has dedicated his life to witchcraft: elevating it, making it better, and making it last. Ivo's work is regurgitation of the texts written by people twenty to one hundred years ago. It is an instruction manual for magick in the future informed by real-world trial and error. It's is what witches will reference twenty to one hundred years in the future. It's a legacy, and we will all benefit from it.

The Four Elements of the Wise is something I desperately needed as a newbie witch; now, as a more seasoned witch, it is something I still desperately need. The elementals are a ubiquitous category in witchcraft. We talk about them so flippantly as to take them for granted, but when pressed, it's quickly apparent that most of us don't actually know what they are. This is not a quick read, nor is it meant to be. It is a book to carefully explore and unpack and is best treated like a workbook or a reference text.

You will find likely yourself returning to it over the years. Take your time with Ivo's words. They are rooted in a lifetime of real-world study and application. As an author, he takes the reader on a journey not made simply of memorized factoids but one that opens the door for witches to enter into an actual relationship with and understanding of the different components of magick. He turns the esoteric, complicated concepts into something highly accessible.

You will find your experiences validated and your questions answered.

You will not find a witch who is deeper in thought, or in love, with re-enchanting the world than Ivo Dominguez, Jr. The magickal world is enriched by his work. By reading this book, your world will be enriched, too.

Enjoy!

—Courtney Weber, August 2020

1

How to Use This Book

There is an abundance of material on the Elements in books, blogs, and oral teachings. Much of the material is aimed at beginners, and quite a bit of it is variations on the same ideas. There is very little at the intermediate level except as references to the Elements that are included to support other work or studies. One of the unfortunate outcomes of this situation is a tendency to underestimate the value of working with the Elements.

It is also easy to come to the mistaken conclusion that there just isn't that much to be learned about them. This is often followed by relegating the Elements to beginners' work or something to be sped through to get on with more important studies. I have been studying and working with the Elements since 1976, and I am still finding qualities that are new to me. More importantly, I am still in awe of the Elements and their place in the universe. It is my hope that this book will encourage you to discover or rediscover the wonder of the Elements.

I am a Wiccan who has studied and trained in several other systems and traditions. This book was written to be accessible and adaptable to a wide range of traditions. Whenever possible, I explain how and why something works rather than giving you lore to be memorized. It is more straightforward to adapt something to your needs if you understand how it works. There may be things that you encounter as you read that aren't part of your magickal areas of interest. I think it is great fun to learn new things. Pause in your reading of this book and jump online or riffle through your shelves to fill in the gaps. In giving the Elements a far-reaching look, quite a bit of territory is covered.

This book is designed to have value to both newcomers and long-timers. Even with the more introductory sections, the approaches taken and the mode of categorization is distinctive. In most of the chapters, there is a mixture of information at different levels aimed at different audiences and backgrounds. Ideally, you will be rereading passages or whole chapters as you work your way through the book to discover all the levels. Like most occult or metaphysical teachings, the knowledge and wisdom are not linear. The ideas are all related to one another, and the order in which they are best understood or what serves as a prerequisite or foundation for that learning is hard to decide. Each of the chapters in the book can be read as stand-alone lessons, but they are meant to be understood in the context of all the chapters.

I don't like writing filler or padding out chapters for the sake of lengthening a book. So, expect to take your time as you read. Please pause and think about what you are reading so that you develop your own ideas and understanding of what is presented. If you are reading this book with some friends or a study group, allow processing and discussion time for each chapter. If you are reading it by yourself, keep notes of any questions or ideas that you may want to reexamine as you work through the book. If you have spells, rituals, or other sorts of workings that involve the Elements that you've done or plan to do, you may wish to collect them and have them at hand. As you read, you may wish to see how the material relates to these workings. Following the last chapter, you will find a short list of suggested books to supplement your studies. You may wish to read these after completing this book or alongside it.

There is quite a bit of variation in how occult terms and vocabulary are used. There is no consensus or agreement on the definitions of many terms, and sometimes the divergence is very large. Wherever it seems needed, I am defining my terms. You need not adopt them in your practices, but keep my usages in mind as you read. My capitalization will not be standard, but that is for the sake of clarity. A *term of art* is a word or group of words that carry precise and unique meaning within a specific field, context, or system. Magick and metaphysics are full of terms of art, and this book has quite a few. Try to add these terms of art to your working memory to help with fully understanding this book.

Every reader has their own reading style and rhythm. Each chapter in this book contains information that gives context and meaning to the chapters later in the book. At times, it may be tempting to skip ahead to something that has attracted your attention. If you skip ahead, however, you may not connect all the dots, and this will hamper your understanding of the material. If there is urgency to read about a particular chapter, try to give a quick skim to the whole book first. This book is meant to be read slowly and with deliberation. There are some exercises and ritual suggestions that I hope you will perform and not merely read. Although parts of this book may be entertaining, it is meant to be studied and lead to an expansion of your practices.

When I was first introduced to the Elements in the context of witchcraft, they were referred to as the Elements of the Wise. This was to remind us that the candle flame, water in the cup, passing breeze, and pebble were representations and proxies for the universal version of the Elements. I was also taught that if you were wise, you would see past the surface of things and see that the Elements exist beyond the physical plane as well. It was also a reminder that a map is not the territory, and a statue is not a deity, though it is useful to have proxies and representations. It is my hope that by the time you have finished reading *The Four Elements of the Wise,* you will have grown wiser about these cornerstones of magick and metaphysics.

2

Core Concepts for
the Elements

*"We have said that there is no religion without mysteries;
let us add that there are no mysteries without symbols. The
symbol, being the formula or the expression of the mystery,
only expresses its unknown depth by paradoxical images
borrowed from the known."*

—Éliphas Lévi, *The Key of the Mysteries*

Before beginning, let's take a step back and gain some perspective
and context, so we can study the Elements with more openness to
all their possibilities. Effective magick uses symbols, placeholders,
frameworks, resonant links, and the flexibility of the human psyche
to engage with powers that are vaster than humanity and with those
that lie hidden within. The Elements themselves are real, but like
other great spiritual potencies and presences, only the smallest frac-
tion of their totality can be perceived in the world of dense matter.
It requires just the right frame of mind, skill, and determination to
use small finite symbols to call for the Elements without overlapping
the boundaries between them and forgetting the enormity that they
represent.

When a beam of white light is split by a prism, it widens into a
band of color that spans the range of colors from red to violet. If the
angle of projection is adjusted, the spectrum expands to show what
is perceived as ever more subtle shifts of color in a seemingly endless
and continual progression of colors. The names that we have for colors
help us to divide the endless into the manageable. Blue contains many

versions and possibilities, but it narrows the field. Names have power, and, in naming a color, you can call upon it. If something is described as blue, you can imagine it more accurately. It also becomes easier for you to communicate with others. You can color code documents; you can give the instruction to only pick the tomatoes when they are red; you can visualize the color that corresponds to energy being raised in a ritual.

A talented singer can take a deep breath and produce a sound that starts low and deep then slide it upward to reach the top of their range. Like the spectrum of the rainbow, sound is experienced as a continuum. To create musical compositions, that spectrum is divided into notes to mark those particular locations, specific frequencies. Both sound and light have frequencies and wavelengths, but there are important differences. Human sight is only sensitive to a narrow range of frequencies in the electromagnetic spectrum. The average range of frequencies that can be heard is broader than that of sight.

When you are looking at something that is yellow, whether it is a pale pastel, bright as a daffodil, or a muddy yellow ochre, it is in a narrow range of frequencies of light that indicate that it is yellow. When you hear a note played on different instruments you can still identify it as the same note, much in the same way that you can identify a color despite changes in hue, tint, tone, and shade. If a piano player starts at the right end of the keyboard, hits a note at a time and continues down the keyboard skipping an octave each time, you will hear a sequence of notes that are the same yet different. The frequencies of the notes are different, but there is a consistent ratio between the notes, so they are experienced as related.

When you work with the Elements, you are accessing some of the primal forces and building blocks that are part and parcel of the ongoing process of creation. Just as sight and hearing have a narrow band of sensitivity compared to the totality of what exists, your capacity to sense the powers of creation is also very narrow. To work more fully with the Elements, you must exceed the limits of your physical and psychic senses by understanding the process of perception. We can imagine that there are notes above and below what we can hear that are related to the ones that we can sense. Our style of hearing can be extrapolated to what is beyond our senses. By understanding our relationship to colors and how they interact with one another, we can project the vastness of what is beyond us and map it onto what falls within our senses.

At the heart of the systems of colors, symbols, magickal tools, correspondences, directional alignments, and so on that are used to call upon the Elements is the assertion that connecting with a small representation of an Element opens a connection to a larger version of that Element. The word "emblems" is my catchall term for these representations of the Elements. The emblems for the Elements can be understood and applied using the perceptual style of any of the senses, but let's keep to the senses of sound and sight for the moment.

When you focus your awareness on a symbol, a key, to an Element, think of it as playing middle C on the piano. That symbol, that key, is one form of that Element. The notes in the octaves above and below can be imagined even if they are not being played. The notes above and below the range of your hearing can also be imagined and intuited. The octaves can be thought of as other planes of being and as the elemental realms that you may access through the power of symbols, imagination, and resonance.

Approached in terms of color, the richness, the saturation, of a color could be used as either a measure of intensity for the presence of an Element or as a way to attract it or concentrate it. For example, if you associate the color red with Fire, then envisioning a bright red may be a way to call the power of Fire through resonance. Envisioning pink, could for example, indicate pure fire energy but diluted by a broad range of other energies for a gentler effect. Different traditions use different symbols and colors for the Elements, but the underlying patterns governing the perception of color are much more universal.

As you explore any current symbol set you use for the Elements or as you add more to your collection of emblems for the Elements, pause to reflect on the way your senses work and how that relates to the conditioning and perspectives built into those systems.

The Value of Using the Elements

The universe has more mysteries, types of energies, sources of power than we can name or imagine. Human thought relies upon words, images, feelings, and so on to shape, to convey, and to punctuate consciousness. It is easier to work with powers if you have some way to conceptualize them and to focus upon them. Human consciousness prefers to seek patterns and summarize experience into stories. Stories require characters, so the process of finding and refining narratives also includes the creation and identification of living beings to enact the narratives. Stories are fuller and feel more real if the background and landscape are well developed, too. The Elements that are used in magick have well-developed symbols, patterns, stories, and characters.

Just because we, as a community of people working with the Elements over many generations, have created and modified the stories, the playbook, the canon for the Elements is not a statement about their objective reality. I believe the Elements are real, as are the God/dess/es and many other beings and forces, but all the icons, names, myths, and so on that we associate with them are our creation. Even the special stories we call history are variable and perspective dependent, but that doesn't mean that the past didn't occur. Our understanding and interpretation of the Elements has changed and will change over time, but they themselves are functionally eternal and infinite.

Because the Elements are among the fundamental building blocks of nature, we can use them to create new things. The Elements are like the four bases that make up DNA's alphabet. Or, if you prefer a musical analogy, they are the notes that you use to compose your magick.

Because the Elements are sets of patterns and of tendencies toward specific actions, they can be used as the equivalent of words in the language of magick. There is also a complex and pervasive network of interrelationships between the Elements, different planes of reality, other forces, and spiritual entities. The Elements act as a portal of communication or entry into this network. For all these reasons, the Elements make solid cornerstones and keystones for the creation of sacred space, such as in the casting of a circle.

Introducing Yourself to the Elements

William Carlos Williams, poet, physician, and careful observer of the world, said, *"No ideas but in things"* in his poem "A Sort of a Song," which speaks to the truth that your ideas are formed from what the senses reveal. To form or refresh your ideas that connect you to the Elements, spend some time with physical proxies for them. A candle flame is not the Element of Fire, but it is recognizable as a spark, or a seed, or a portion, or a child, or some relative of the universal Fire.

The same can be said for a vessel filled with water, a stone, or a fan or feathers as stand-ins for the other Elements. Repeated observations and experiences are needed to convert perceptions into fully enlivened ideas. Whether you have worked extensively with the Elements or have just begun your work with them, it is a good practice to period-ically reintroduce yourself to the Elements through physical proxies.

First, collect suitable tangible representatives for the Elements.

- For the Element of Fire, a candle is the most easily obtained, but an oil lamp, fireplace, or something comparable may also be used.
- A vessel filled with water can serve as a proxy for the Element of Water, but you may find that glass or light-colored containers are more effective.
- For Air, I prefer to open a window or sit outside and focus on the wind. This is not always practical, as there may be no wind,

or the weather might be too cold or wet. You may use feathers, a folding fan, or something similar as a substitute. Electric fans or other power fans tend not to work as well for this purpose as those powered by your own hand.

- For Earth, you may wish to use a stone, a crystal, or perhaps a small dish filled with soil. Going outdoors and sitting with Earth in nature may be less effective than working with a sample of earth. When outdoors, it may be hard to single out and identify the Earth energy from the energies of plant and animal life, the flow of the other Elements, and so on. The Element of Earth has a quieter nature than the others, at least until it is awakened.

Plan on spending five to ten minutes with each proxy for the Elements. You may do all four in one session or one at a time over the course of several days. The process is almost the same for each Element. I suggest using a table and chair so that you may sit during the contemplative part of the exercise. It is useful to keep notes of your experiences. If you are not inclined to keep a journal, consider keeping notes on your phone, tablet, or computer. For the purposes of this exercise, refrain from making any invocations, prayers, and so on. The goal is to focus on the physical proxies of the Elements, so do not call upon other forces or beings. You may wish to reread the instructions immediately before each exercise.

Fire

For safety's sake, place the candle, or whatever you are using for a flame, on a plate, metal tray, or some other fireproof surface. Light the candle; use all your senses to observe the flame and to know it deeply, as if you were meeting a person. Listen to the sound of the lighting of the flame and the subtle sounds that follow. Pay careful attention to the shifting shapes and colors of the flame. Gently sniff the air and take notice of the scent of the burning. Bring your hand near the flame and feel the warmth. If you feel comfortable doing so, quickly flick a finger through the flame. You may wish to stand or move about to view the flame from different vantage points. Then sit quietly and focus on what you feel within yourself while you are near the flame. When you are done, snuff out the candle.

Water

Pour water into a bowl or goblet from a pitcher or a faucet. Listen to the sound of the water falling and filling the vessel. Look at the way light moves with the falling and filling. Place the bowl on a table and look into it. Touch the surface of the water and move your fingers through it. Feel the temperature and the texture of the water. You may wish to stand or move about to view the water from different vantage points. Then sit quietly and focus on what you feel within yourself while you are near the water. When you are done, pour the water down the sink. Another option is to take it outdoors as an offering to the land.

Air

Place a folding fan or feathers on a table. Take a few deep breaths; slowly exhale through your mouth each time. Pay attention to the feeling and the sound of breath in motion. Pick up the fan and move it through the air at different speeds and angles. Concentrate on the feeling of the air moving, resisting, and shifting. Listen to the sounds as well. Then turn the fan so that you can feel a breeze on your face and then your arm. Does it feel cool? Can you feel hairs moving? Then sit quietly and focus on what you just experienced. Lastly, take three deep breaths, slowly exhaling through your mouth. Again, pay attention to the feeling and the sound of breath in motion. Hold your breath for a moment on the third breath, find the still Air within you, then release it. Return to a normal pattern of breathing to end the exercise.

Earth

Place a stone, a crystal, or perhaps a small dish filled with soil on a table. Take a few steps back, then slowly approach the Earth proxy. Pay attention to the small details that come into view the closer you get. If possible, lean down even closer so that you can see fine grain texture. Run your fingers across the stone, crystal, or soil and feel the texture and temperature. Push your finger against it and feel its density and resistance. If you are working with soil, breathe in the smell of the earth. Pick up the Earth proxy and slowly move it back and forth to feel its heft. Then sit down and hold it so that you can feel its weight against your hand or leg. Close your eyes and contemplate the presence of Earth. When you are done, keep your mind on the sensations in your body as you stand and place the proxy back onto the table.

Before repeating any of the elemental proxy exercises, read whatever notes you took from the previous efforts. At the very least, repeat these exercises when you reach the middle and the end of this book to observe the differences and additional qualities that you notice. You may certainly do the exercises more often than that if you desire. After you have done them by yourself, you may also compare notes with friends who are also learning about the Elements. It is best to have your own perceptions first to avoid being influenced by another person's description of their experience.

Essential Characteristics

"Spirit is ceaseless and eternal activity. The infinite varieties of this energy are called forces. Every force evolves a form. In fact, a form is only a crystallized force, so much arrested as to become outwardly visible."

—Oliver C. Hampton in "Forces and Forms,"
The Shaker Manifesto, Volumes 22–23 (1892)

More often than not, lessons about the Elements start off with an inventory of characteristics associated with each Element. This enumeration of qualities is mostly a list of human traits, which can result in a quicker entry to understanding the Elements, but it can also encourage a habit of narrower perspectives about them. We'll begin with descriptions that are not anchored in portions of human personality.

The Elements manifest themselves as a spectrum of expressions that spans a wide range of the planes of reality. They exist in myriad detailed and unique iterations in the physical plane and increasingly abstracted and unified forms in higher planes. Ultimately, truly *knowing* the Elements in their higher forms requires elevating your consciousness to those levels while remaining lucid and aware. Until that is possible for you on a regular and consistent basis, working with *descriptions* of higher plane versions of the Elements can be an excellent starting point.

The following are descriptions of the Four Elements as collections of tendencies and first principles. Read them now, but please make time to contemplate them later. One method is to read each description one sentence at a time. Pause and think about what each sentence means, and allow images to form in your mind that illustrate the meaning and action. After you've finished the paragraph, read it again without pauses, and just think about it as a whole. You may do all four in one session or spread them out over time. It is preferable to follow the order of Fire, Water, Air, then Earth for this exercise. This sequence represents the succession of the Elements as they differentiated out of the unity of spirit.

Fire

Fire is called the *ascending force* because its first tendency is to attempt to rise up the planes of reality. More generally, Fire moves up from dense planes of being, up gravity wells, up gradients of subtle energy and subtle matter, and toward the highest plane of being. Fire gives off its own light; it is a bright force, a generative force. Fire's shape and size and intensity can transform readily. Fire is subtle, and its density is highly variable. Its motions can be slow or swift, and every combination of these.

Water

Water is called the **descending force** because its first tendency is to seek the lowest planes of reality. Water is drawn to density and thus matter, as its nature is magnetic. Water is a condensing force that contains within itself the essence of all the attractive forces such as gravity, charge, magnetism, and so on. Water does not produce its own light; it reshapes and pulls and bends light through reflection, transmission, and refraction. Water moves and changes shape with ease, and it adjusts its forms to match its environment. Water has texture and substance, of a sort, at every level of its existence.

Air

Air is called the **distributive force** because its tendency is to move and to spread through all planes of reality. The majority of Air's motive power is directed horizontally, though it may move up or down as well. Air expands and diffuses to fill the space that is available. Air does not produce its own light, but it conveys light and acts as an agent for Fire and Water to interact through light. Air is more rarefied than Water but less subtle than Fire. Its substance is felt mostly as a measure of its motion. Rarefied and subtle are more than references to *density* or other physical attributes. Rarefied in this context means the proportion of form expressed by the Element in the physical plane. Similarly, *subtle* means the proportion of force expressed by the Element in the physical plane.

Earth

Earth is called the *compressive force* because its prime tendency is to become denser. It can also be called the concentrating force because it brings things together. Earth is the crystallizing force because it sorts qualities and shapes and binds them together into stable forms. Earth does not produce its own light, but it can block, absorb, or reflect light. With the exception of motion caused by the forces of compression and crystallization, Earth is more moved by other forces than by its own actions. That said, Earth's hidden power is to anchor and bind—from the smallest to the largest of manifest things.

The Fifth Element

In Western cosmology, the Fifth Element is most often called Spirit, Ether, or Quintessence, though there are other terms as well. These terms are often used interchangeably, but, in truth, they are not identical in meaning. There is a chapter later in this book that will explore these distinctions fully. For now, think of the Fifth Element as the principle of unity and differentiation and as the power of transmutation. The Fifth Element is the fascia, mycelial network, the web, and the weft and warp of creation. It is through the Fifth Element that the Elements may know themselves and others.

Without, Within, and Throughout

The Elements can be viewed at the macro level as the ubiquitous and ever-present building components that make up the universe. It is important to remember that the Elements are both forces and forms, and the transitions between them both subtle and dense. If you look at the ocean, a mountain, the sky, or the sun, you may be moved by the immensity of the Elements in these forms. The challenge of perceiving the Elements at the macro level is that the vastness of the universe is beyond the capacities of your senses and greater than the scope of your consciousness.

In the same way that a panoramic view can be stitched together from multiple photographs, you can become aware that each of the grandest observations of the universal Elements that you've experienced is but a pixel in a panorama. If all the perceptions of all the inhabitants of this planet were pieced together, it would still be a small detail within one photograph.

Looking for the Elements within yourself is considerably easier, but there are still some challenges. The first is that the Elements are more than what you can think or feel about yourself. It is easy to center your attention on how the Elements make themselves known through your personality. It is valuable to be aware of this, but it can lull you into thinking that you know the Elements within when there is more to be learned.

Spend some time in a quiet place with your eyes shut, and open your awareness to the Elements within. Try to quiet the dialogue in your mind until you are finished with this inward journey, then write up some notes about what you learned. The Elements function through time, as well. Consider how the Elements express themselves through metabolism, the process of birth, the process of aging, and so on. Finding the Elements within parallels the work of clearing the mind through mediation, contemplation, and self-discovery.

The Elements are in circulation, within the self, in the greater world, between the within and without and more. The Elements traverse the various planes of reality and remain themselves, though they are transformed to adapt to the density and frequency of each plane. Just as physical water can be a solid, a liquid, a gas, or a plasma, the Elements also have something akin to phase shifts in different planes of reality. Like calls to like, and the Elements resonate with and call to each of their instantiations, their equivalents of incarnations.

Everywhere and everywhen throughout manifest reality, the Elements, as forces and forms, are present as their equivalent of instance objects, as seemingly separate entities based on a common pattern. The Elements are responsible for much of what holds the manifest reality together as a unity. When you work magick of any sort, and particularly elemental magick, it is in part through accessing this web, root-mass, and network that is made of the elemental relationships.

As you read more about the emblems, particular details, color symbolism, practical applications, et cetera, about the Elements, do not let the ideas in this chapter fade into the background. When you are calling the Elements, you are doing so with your psyche and the Elements within yourself. The more fully and deeply you understand the Elements, the more powerfully and exact will be their contribution to your work. Additionally, realizing how and why the Elements work will give you the capacity to adjust existing spells or workings or create new ones.

3

The Fundamental Lore

Historical Background

A proper history of the development of the doctrine of the Elements and their relationship to occultism and metaphysics in Western magick would probably require a book thicker than the *Oxford Dictionary of English*. If we included elemental theories and arrangements from the rest of the world, nothing less than an encyclopedia would suffice. Hopefully, the few paragraphs that follow will be a good introduction that will inspire you to look deeper into the history of these ideas.

The Four Elements system that is most prevalent in modern magick was clarified and refined by Empedocles of Acragas sometime around 450 BCE in his long poem "On Nature." Empedocles did not create the Four Elements system, but he did take what he had been taught by the Pythagoreans and other schools of thought and expand upon them by proposing patterns of relationships between the Elements. He called Fire, Water, Air, and Earth the four roots, the fundaments, from which all things came into being. Later on, it was Plato who called them "elements," and it was Aristotle who added the Fifth Element of Aether.

Until some other older writings are discovered, Empedocles' poem marks the beginning of the Elements as a system that is central to many forms of magick and to sacred sciences such as astrology and alchemy. Among his other deep insights, he had his own theory of natural selection, asserted that light had a finite speed, and his Elements theory had its own version of the law of conservation of mass. He also taught that the Elements, which are eternal essences, came into being in a whirling void and condensed into the Earth. The forces that drive the ever-changing Elements he named "love" and "strife." Later we will explore those forces under the names of "evolution" and "involution."

Around 400 BCE, the great physician Hippocrates of Kos taught that illness was caused by natural causes, among them an imbalance of the Elements. The "four humors" were the Elements as identified as fluids in the body:

- Air as blood,
- Fire as yellow bile,
- Earth as black bile, and
- Water as phlegm.

Later, around 170 CE, Galen of Pergamon proposed the four temperamental classes—called sanguine, choleric, melancholic, and phlegmatic—after the humors. Galen was one of the early proponents of the mind-body connection in health, and this is an early form of the Elements being associated with personality traits.

In 1025 CE, the great polymath Avicenna (Ibn Sīnā) of Persia significantly expanded these concepts in his *Canon of Medicine*. There were a great many others who continued to explore the Elements as they expressed in their fields. In the 20th century, the fourfold nature of the Elements became one of the core inspirations for Carl Gustav Jung, whose work, in turn, has shaped many modern metaphysical concepts.

At the same time that the Elements were working their way through the centuries in the fields of philosophy, medicine, and psychology, they were also being integrated into the core sacred sciences of Western magick. It was Alexander the Great's conquests in 331 BCE that accelerated the mixing of teachings from Mesopotamia and Egypt with Greek ideas that resulted in the root of Western astrology that is used today. This is when the Elements became the building blocks of astrology.

If you remove the framework of the Elements, it is very hard to do the great work of alchemy. In 1605, the Polish alchemist Michal

Sedziwoj, also known as Sendivogius, wrote in his work *Novum Lumen Chymicum*:

> There are four common elements, and each has at its center another deeper element which makes it what it is. These are the four pillars of the world. They were in the beginning evolved and molded out of chaos by the hand of the Creator; and it is their contrary action which keeps up the harmony and equilibrium of the mundane machinery of the universe; it is they, which through the virtue of celestial influences, produce all things above and beneath the earth.

We will explore quite a few of the ideas in this quote throughout this book. I encourage you to reread this quote before continuing.

The teachings of both the traditional Kabbalah and the Hermetic Qabala are rich with the fourfold pattern of the Elements. The Elements appear in Kabbalistic books, such as the *Zohar*, *Sefer Yetzira*, *Midrash*, and *Sha'are Orah*, as well as in many Hassidic teachings. Alchemy and Qabala, as well as Islam, Neo-Platonism, and Hermetics crossed paths in Spain in the mid to late 13th century, setting the stage for the Renaissance revival of magick. From the 15th century onward, beginning in Florence with Marcelio Ficino, we see magicians making contributions to the expansion of the Qabala. This is the birth of the Hermetic Tree.

Many others followed, such as Cornelius Agrippa, Johannes Reuchlin, and Francis Barrett. In the 19th century, Papus (Gérard Encausse) and Éliphas Lévi (Alphonse Louis Constant), inextricably connected the Tree to the tarot. In the 19th century, the explosion of interest and organizations such as the Hermetic Order of the Golden Dawn promoted the version of the Hermetic Qabala as we know it today. All tarot decks that follow the template of the Rider-Waite-Colman Smith deck are built upon the symbolism of the Four Elements and the Hermetic Qabala.

Looking through the books on my shelves, I can find twenty or so variations for spelling Qabala. The most common variations are Kabbalah, Cabala, and Qabalah. In most, but not all, cases, the "K" spellings are associated with Judaism, the "C" spellings are associated with Christianity, and the "Q" spellings with occultism. An easy way to remember this is "K" is for kosher, "C" is for Christ, and "Q" is for the trans-dimensional being from *Star Trek*. Once, this was a good way to guess at the starting premises and perspective of a book on the tree of life, but these distinctions have gotten blurred by the use of the spellings as alternatives rather than signifiers. The variations in the doubling of the letter "b" or "l" and the inclusion of "h" at the end are attempts to suggest the pronunciation and which syllable to emphasize. My preferred spelling is Qabala for its brevity and the magickal rather than religious associations.

Somewhen deep in time, humans began to recognize that plants, animals, rivers, storms, and everything that could be observed or named had its own spiritual nature and will. Some variation or combination of animism, pantheism, and polytheism can be found at the roots of most cultures. Indeed, there are many vibrant, living cultures present today that are still true to these roots. There are a vast number of names, attributes, categories, and stories to describe these myriad beings. Some of these beings are strongly connected to Fire, Water, Air, or Earth in that they appear to primarily consist of that Element, but that does not mean they are elementals. The spirit that you perceive in a river may be a nature spirit rather than an elemental.

Nature spirits come in many forms, but they all tend to be a blend of essences and substances, including but not limited to the Elements. A river spirit, for example, may be the summation of the living beings in the water and the land through which it courses. Elementals of various sorts may be a part of a river spirit as well. The category of elemental can mean a wide range of things in different systems of magick, but in this book we will only apply it to beings whose *spirit* is of a single Element. Please note that this definition differs from some other authors' teachings, as it affirms that elementals have spirit. For example, Paracelsus believed that elementals did not possess an immortal soul.

Elementals are divided into four classes of beings.
- The salamanders are the beings of Fire.
- The sylphs are the beings of the Air.
- The undines are the beings of Water.
- The gnomes are the beings of Earth.

These classes of beings were given these names by Swiss alchemist Paracelsus in the 16th century. He also described their qualities and appearances in *Liber de Nymphis*. The imprint of his view on the nature of elementals is still present in many systems of magick in use today. Agrippa had written about elementals decades earlier than Paracelsus, who was influenced by Agrippa, but by naming the elementals, Paracelsus made a more lasting impression on the storehouse of magickal images. There is great power in names and naming.

A Focused Approach

There are dozens upon dozens of popular systems for describing and representing the Elements. There are many more that are rare and less easily encountered. Those systems that are the creations of specific cultures, spiritual traditions, or serious practitioners are self-consistent and workable. Each is worthy of study and application, but the goal of this book is to give you enough so that you can work with the Elements competently. Rather than give you one bite from each dish on a smorgasbord of elemental systems, I'll offer the one I know best.

While it is valuable to study multiple systems, you must be able to give each one their proper time and space in your mind. Trying to study too many at once can result in a garbled understanding.

Moreover, it is important that you not force-fit one model of the Elements onto another. Though systems for the Elements may be similar in that they focus on fundamental building blocks of nature, their paradigms and scales of measurement can make comparisons and the suggestion of analogous categories unreasonable. It's not a question of apples and oranges, that at least share the category of fruit, but more like comparing fish and algae because they both live in water.

The model for the Elements that I am presenting will look familiar to those who have a background in Western magick, wicca, and many other forms of modern paganism. The schema for the Elements in this book is the one that is taught in the Assembly of the Sacred Wheel. I will make an effort to point out when it is a significant change from the more mainstream perspectives on the Elements.

The Elements in the Personality

Air

The powers of thought and communication belong to the Element of Air. Air expresses itself in our ability to use our senses and in our capacity for imagination. Air can pick up and transport water vapor, dust, pollen, and more. Sound, light, temperatures, electric charges, and other types of energy, including spiritual energies, are also conveyed by Air. The mind and its stream of consciousness is better thought of as a swirling, changing weather pattern than as a river.

The word inspiration is derived from Latin and means to breathe in or blow into, and that is also a gift of Air. Bursts of creativity in the arts or in spiritual matters are also in Air's domain. The challenge of Air is to accept differences of thought, truths, and convictions within themselves and others. Air corresponds to the sanguine humor. Thus, it is associated with traits such as adaptability, innovation, social influence, and a desire for activity.

Fire

The powers of desire, resolve, and purpose belong to the Element of Fire. Fire is the force of directed consciousness expressed as will and fed by passion. Fire generates its own light and heat and moves constantly as it seeks to rise. As such, Fire corresponds to the soul, which also is self-radiant and seeks the source of all things.

At the level that Fire exists within the human psyche, it also needs fuel to burn, and that need is the root of passion and desire. Will, in all its forms from its lowest to its highest manifestations, is a manifestation of Fire within the psyche. Fire also gives impetus to the longings of your soul and to the work of your life. The challenge of Fire is to redirect frustration and anger so that they serve the purposes of your will. Fire corresponds to the choleric humor. As such, it is associated with traits such as boldness, quick action, passion, and ambition.

Water

The powers of the emotions, sensitivity to others, a sense of mystic unity, cycles of change, and transformation belong to the Element of Water. Water both takes the shape of its surroundings and changes the shape of its surroundings. In Water, there is the often overlooked strength that springs from vulnerability and authenticity. It is all the unseen that lies beneath the surface of waking consciousness that turns the tides of awareness.

The meaning and appreciation of life is in the domain of Water. The capacity to trust and to take a risk arises from the deep sense of connection to the universe that is Water's gift. The challenge of Water is to find serenity and to stay present with your emotions. Water corresponds to the phlegmatic humor. As such, it is associated with traits such as peace seeking, understanding, empathy, and emotional intelligence.

Earth

The powers of the instinct, organization, stability, fertility, and manifestation belong to the Element of Earth. The joy of sensuality, of being in a body, is one of the gifts of Earth. The healing and the wisdom of the body come from Earth being all the structures from the smallest to the largest. Boundaries, both physical and psychological, are in the domain of Earth. This is the Element of protection, anchoring, and steadiness. Your awareness of the passage of time and the experience of moving through your life is also an expression of the Element of Earth.

The challenge of Earth is to find centeredness by balancing achievement with service to others. Earth corresponds to the melancholic humor. As such, it is associated with traits such as introspection, practicality, quiet power, and guardianship.

The Four Powers of the Magus

Alphonse Louis Constant, who wrote as Éliphas Lévi, is, as far as we know, the first author to clearly formulate the four powers of the magus as a canon for the development of a magician's capabilities and discernment. He named these four powers as: to know, to dare, to will, to keep silence. These are also referred to as the four powers of the sphinx because one form of the sphinx is an amalgamation of a lion, an eagle, a human, and a bull, which refer to the four fixed signs of the zodiac and the four elements.

In the four powers of the magus, Air is the power to know, Fire is the power to will, Water is the power to dare, Earth is the power to be silent. This is also in alignment with the four holy living creatures, cherubim, and lamassu, and we'll return to this topic later in this book. When all four powers, styles of consciousness, modes of life, and so on, are brought into enlivened and active union within yourself, you are sovereign within the holy kingdom of your spirit.

There is a fifth power implied by this union of the four. Aleister Crowley, the founder of Thelema, named a fifth power as the power to go. The fifth power is correlated to Spirit, also known as Quintessence or Ether. The addition of a fifth power, one that implied motion and a higher vibration or plane, fed the collective imagination and gave rise to the construct of the Witches' Pyramid. Four equidistant points and a fifth above implied the shape of a pyramid and was also reminiscent of a cone of power.

It is unclear when the concept of the Witches' Pyramid was created, but it has been in fairly wide usage since the 1960s (Leo Louis Martello's teachings were my first exposure) and became widespread in the 1970s through the writings of Paul Huson and Lady Sheba. In the pagan community, in addition to being used as a tool for personal development, the Witches' Pyramid became a template for spellwork and operative magick.

The descriptions for the four powers of the magus, the Witches' Pyramid, can vary a bit from tradition to tradition, but they are all extensions of how the Elements express in the human psyche. There are also debates about which Element is assigned to which power with good rationales on all sides. Whenever you read these descriptions or any other metaphysical teachings, including that which you already hold as true, apply some of science fiction writer Theodore Sturgeon's credos. He often stated, "Nothing is always absolutely so." Theodore Sturgeon's love of deep thinking also caused him to encourage everyone to, "Ask the next question." He created a sigil that was the letter "Q" with an arrow through it that was a reminder to never stop asking questions and to follow up those questions with more questions. Through this process, an understanding that is ever closer to accurate may be obtained. He was often seen wearing a pendant with this sigil as a reminder.

Colors

Color associations are a powerful tool for working with the Elements. Gazing upon or visualizing a color is a quick way to begin to align yourself with an Element. Color coding is useful in selecting the particular color for a candle, an altar cloth, or other ritual items for calling or focusing a particular Element into a working. What is not useful is believing that one system is more correct than another system. It is also problematic to dismiss established systems of color associations and decide that the color for Water is orange in today's working and is pink tomorrow.

Systems of associations and correlations are useful as containers, notation, focal points, way-finders to power and act as mechanisms to bridge the physical with the subtle. The use of colors linked to the Elements, or other symbols or representations, allows the imagination to engage the gears of the engine of the universe to make magick.

The most prevalent color arrangement that you'll encounter is likely to be:

- Air ≈ yellow
- Fire ≈ red
- Water ≈ blue
- Earth ≈ green

The Hermetic Order of the Golden Dawn used this arrangement of colors, and their teachings were used as source material for many traditions that are widespread today. Sometimes you'll see a variation from this pattern, with Earth being color coded as brown or black. The color arrangement I use is Air ≈ blue, Fire ≈ red, Water ≈ white or silver, and Earth ≈ yellow or gold.

- If you have been using another system of colors and are firmly invested in it, then it is probably better that you continue using it.
- If you join a tradition that uses something different or want to add another set of associations to your practices, use the new one without returning to the old one for at least several months.

Think of it as being similar to trying to learn variant lyrics to a well-loved folk song. If you want to be able to sing either version on demand, they both need to be ingrained in memory as separate, despite sharing melodic characteristics.

Oftentimes, the choices of specific colors for the Elements are justified by looking to see how they manifest in nature. For example, Water is identified as blue because of the beauty of brilliant blue lakes and the majesty of blue seas. Looking to the great book of nature as a definitive source is fraught with same problems as looking to sacred texts for definitive answers. You can generally find and interpret a verse or a passage to mean whatever you want it to mean, and you can find another bit of holy writ to contradict or modify the first.

If you look at Water in nature, it may be transparent, or the bright flash of light reflecting upon its surface, or the color of its container, or the reflection of its surroundings, or colored by what is carried or dissolved within it. How many colors does fire have? Once you have settled on working with a set of color associations, then the value of knowing and collecting images and stories about why a color is assigned to an Element is about deepening the connection between the two in your mind.

Symbols

Figures, glyphs, and simple symbols that can be easily visualized, scribed with energy, marked on objects, and so on, are among the most direct and effective means to attract and anchor the Elements for spiritual and magickal purposes. There are a multitude of depictions for the Elements, each with their own value and best uses. The special value of symbols is in their minimalism. It is easier to hold a simple shape in your mind. A pared down and elegant symbol is less distracting when used as a focus for meditation or a target to receive energy.

More elaborate representations of the Elements are the proper tools for teaching processes and cycles, specifying the aspects of the

Element that you wish to emerge, enacting multiple purposes, and more that will be explored later. As a general principle in magick, simple symbols are more inclusive and expansive and relate to the higher plane version of whatever they represent. Intricate depictions call forth more specific and definite versions of whatever they represent and are lower plane expressions.

Triangles

The symbols for the Elements that are based on triangles primarily come to modern occultism through alchemical symbols from the 16th century. The origins for these triangular symbols for the Elements are older and connected to multiple cultures. Triangles are the simplest polygon, needing only three points to define them. They certainly meet the simplicity rule for ease of visualization.

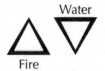

Water

Fire

A triangle pointing upwards represents the Element of Fire, because its nature is to rise. A triangle pointing downwards represents the Element of Water, because its nature is to descend. Fire and Water can be thought of as opposites, contrasts, complements to each other. Fire is bright and subtle, while Water is dark and dense. When they are overlapped, it represents a sacred union that produces the Elements of Air and Earth. The illustration of this union shows Water as gray to make it easier to see the derivation of the symbols.

Fire + Water

The symbol for Air is a triangle with a horizontal line through its upper quarter. Air is the child of Fire and Water that inherited more qualities of Fire than Water. Fire's upward motion has become expanding and distributive in Air with the addition of a bit of Water. Air is denser than Fire but still very mobile. The symbol for Earth is a triangle with a horizontal line through its lower quarter. Earth is the child of Water and Fire that inherited more qualities of Water than Fire. Water's downward motion becomes compressing and crystallizing with the additional motive force of Fire.

Air   Earth

The hexagram, the six-pointed star, can also be seen as the Elements in balance. This shape is also referred to as the Shield of David, one of the forms of the Seal of Solomon, and the Shatkona which is the union of Shakti and Shiva (or Purusha and Prakriti). It is not surprising that many cultures use this shape as a symbol, because it is a primal geometric form. What is intriguing is that the hexagram often represents power that arises from creating wholeness in cultures that have had little cultural exchange with one another.

I have found that the hexagram can be used as a focus for contemplating the Elements and their interrelationships. This shape has roots deep in the collective consciousness of humanity, so before using it as a focal point for the Elements, be sure to clear away its other symbiolic meanings. Trace the symbols of the four Elements with your eye or with your finger to attune the hexagram before using it as an elemental focus. Then, you may use it to deepen your connection to these symbols for the Elements.

Tattvas

"The universe came out of tatwa or the tatwas; it goes on by the instrumentality of the tatwas; it disappears in the tatwas; by the tatwas is known the nature of the universe."

—Rama Prasad, quoting the *Sivagama*

The Sanskrit word *tattva* can be translated as meaning thatness, evolute, essence, principle, and a host of other similar words. This resonates strongly to the multiple meanings that we have for the term "Element" in the West. It can also be spelled as tattwa, tatvva, and tatwa. Early concepts on the tattvas are found in *Samkhyakarika* in the 4th century CE though the root ideas are present in Hindu philosophy in the 2nd century BCE. It should be noted that in an ancient cultures, ideas have often been active parts of their practices for centuries before they are codified and recorded.

Rama Prasad's book *The Science of Breath and the Philosophy of the Tattwas* (1890) was very influential in the adoption of the tattvas into Theosophy and also into the Hermetic Order of the Golden Dawn. Material on the tattvas becomes a part of the Golden Dawn's teachings at least as early as 1894.

The Theosophical Society and the Golden Dawn are perhaps the two largest shapers of what we now call the Western magickal or Western mystery tradition.

In the 1930s, Franz Bardon incorporated the tattvas into his system of magick as taught in his book, *Initiation into Hermetics*. In the West, especially in ceremonial magick, the tattva symbols are used in meditation and visualization to deepen one's connection to the Elements and to awaken psychic skills. The tattvas are can be used for many more magickal and spiritual purposes as well. The tattva symbols have accumulated a considerable store of energy, information, and essence from the many groups and individuals that have used them over their long history. They exist as highly refined and empowered forms on the other planes of being.

Although the tattvas can be worked as simple geometric forms, they also have specific colors associated with them. The combination of a shape with a color make for particularly strong mental anchors for these symbols. The tattva for Air is represented by a blue circle that suggests the blue dome of the encircling winds of heavens. The tattva for Fire is represented by a red triangle that calls to mind a stylized flame, sharp edged with the bite of fire. The tattva for Water is represented by a silver crescent that tells us that water has no color, reflects light, and is both the tides and the tug of the moon. The tattva for Earth is represented by a yellow square, yellow for gold (the highest vibration of matter) and the rectilinear solidity of a square with the echo of the four quarters in its form. Spirit, the union of Elements, is represented by an egg that may be black, clear, or all colors at once. The yellow square of Earth can also be represented as gold in color. The crescent of Water can also be represented as a pale gray, nearly white.

The Tattva Symbols

The Correlations To The Parts Of Self Are Not Traditional

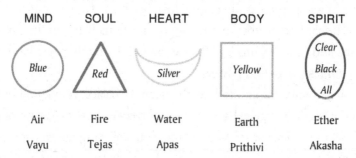

MIND	SOUL	HEART	BODY	SPIRIT
Blue	Red	Silver	Yellow	Clear Black All
Air	Fire	Water	Earth	Ether
Vayu	Tejas	Apas	Prithivi	Akasha

In the Assembly of the Sacred Wheel, we also associate the Elements with what we call the five holy parts of self, and we use the tattvas as the primary symbols for these.

- Air is associated with the mind and the blue circle.
- Fire is associated with the soul and the red triangle.
- Water is associated with the heart and the silver crescent.
- Earth is associated with the body and the yellow square.
- Ether is associated with the egg of all colors and the spirit.

For the sake of clarity, the term "soul" in this context refers to the spiritual essence that is attached to the physical plane through incarnation. The term "spirit" in this context is the eternal and more expansive spiritual essence that is not bounded by linear time and space.

The Cardinal Directions and More

The four Elements are assigned to the cardinal directions—the primary compass points—by numerous cultures and systems of magick. They vary depending upon how and why those assignments were made. The choices may have been determined in accordance with mythology, geographical features, or personal or collective gnosis, and these assignments work within their context and cultural framework. The Elements are everywhere and in everything on the physical plane of existence. The Elements and their realms of origin do not reside nor arise in any particular direction. However, it is advantageous to create directional frameworks to open up connections between the physical plane and other realms by offering the mind a mythopoeic landscape that unites places and powers.

In a similar fashion to how the memory palace, or method of loci, can be used to augment the powers of recollection by placing objects or ideas in an imaginary location that you walk through in your mind, aligning the Elements with directions that are in turn connected to other magickal concepts allows a great amount of lore to be accessed and used.

The correlations of east to Air, south to Fire, west to Water, north to Earth, and the center to Spirit/Ether are the most widespread in modern paganism. It is also the pattern used in casting a circle in many systems. That would be a good enough reason to use this arrangement, but it also dovetails neatly into other systems such as astrology and Hermetic Qabala, which expands the reach of the interlocking ideas.

In an astrological chart, the cardinal directions are flipped so that south is on the top and east is on the left. The diagram showing the correlations between the directions, the Elements, and times is arranged like an astrological chart. It will be important to remain flexible and alert to changes in orientation and direction of motion as we explore how the Elements interact in different planes of being and frames of reference. Directions, bearings, clockwise, and counterclockwise are a matter of perspective. I suggest you study these charts until you know these associations by heart.

If you have some background in Hermetic Qabala, the next bit will sink in more quickly and clearly; if not, then consider this a part of your introduction. In the tree of life, the sphere for the plane of physical reality is called Malkuth and can be represented by a quartered circle. This quartered circle is four earth tones, with yellow ochre on the top, russet on the left, olive on the right, and black on the bottom. Each sphere on the tree of life contains the pattern of the whole tree. The Elements are also present in Malkuth, and each occupy one of the quarters. When a circle is cast, we start in the physical plane and rise and/or expand into other planes.

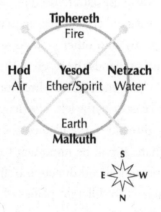

The most widespread method of casting a circle takes your awareness between the worlds to begin the work in the astral plane. It does so in part by being a reflection of the tree, and, like the wheel of the astrological chart, it is also inverted and flipped when compared to the directions of the physical plane. The powers of the Elements are acknowledged, the three pillars on the tree are referenced, and the center of the circle leads to the ways above and below.

For some of you, this would be a good time to pause and match up your knowledge and thoughts on the Hermetic tree with these connections to circle casting. If the Qabala is new to you, then just hang on to the idea that the calling of the quarters, of the Elements, starts here on earth and proceeds higher, changing as it goes.

The ideas in this chapter will be expanded upon and connected to other ideas as you proceed in this book. If you are new to this material, you may wish to reread this chapter before continuing onward. You may also wish to draw and color the tattva symbols and the triangular symbols for the Elements. This can be doodling, or you may feel inspired to make altar pieces or small banners. The process of using your own hands to create these symbols in a tangible way helps to make the learning stick.

4

Spirits of the Elements

Elemental Consciousness

Early in my training as a witch and as a magician, I was taught that one of the defining traits of being human was having a fourfold nature and a soul/spirit. The Elements each have a style of perception and consciousness in addition to their energy, and these four modes are blended in human consciousness. Over the years, I have come to the conclusion that all physically incarnated beings that are alive also partake of the fourfold nature, not just humans. On the physical plane, the Four Elements are ubiquitous, and the subtle and the dense are intertwined. Like calls to like, so the presence of the physical Elements summons their subtle equivalents. Physical beings that have consciousness and/or self-awareness also have a threefold nature in some variation akin to the lower, middle, and higher selves.

Beings that do not have physical bodies may have any combination of the fourfold and the threefold natures running the full gamut, from a complete set to just one from each of the natures. Nonetheless, whether made of dense matter or subtle matter, all beings that have shapes and characteristics exist within the manifest universe. Everything that exists within the manifest universe has a pattern of relationships and interactions with the universe and everything within it. The beings that have the full complement of the fourfold and threefold natures tend to be microcosms of the whole, the macrocosm. This falls in line with the Hermetic axiom of "as above so below" and is a more explicit rendering of the idea of being made in the image of the divine.

Beings that have a subset of the fourfold and threefold natures tend to act as *holons*, a term coined by philosopher Arthur Koestler in 1967. Holons have qualities of wholeness and self-existence, as well as being parts that are subordinated to a larger structure. For example, lungs are identifiable as specialized and unique, but also a part of a body. Atoms make up a compound, and each has its own existence, but are related in a tiered order with atoms being a component within a compound. Elementals are more like holons than they are like microscosms. Elementals also interact with each other, and the rest of the universe, in a mutual and rhizomatic manner.

In botany, a rhizome is an underground stem that spreads horizontally and can put out roots or shoots as needed. Each part of the rhizome has the potential to become a separate plant. Often a stand of what looks like a clump of plants is actually one plant with many shoots arising from a rhizome. The network of interconnections between many rhizomes is nonhierarchical as is the map of connections between elementals.

The beings who are commonly identified as elementals have subtle bodies and spirits that are composed overwhelmingly of one Element. They are not 100 percent of one Element, because for them to exist, experience, and interact with manifest reality, they need at the minimum two more components. Elementals have a small imprint, a seed, of the pattern of the other three Elements within themselves that shapes their inevitable and necessary interactions with elementals that are not of their home Element. Moreover, they have a spark of the spirit of their home Element that is also a reflection of the quintessence. This is how the Elements in general, and elementals in particular, navigate and map their existence within the larger framework of the macrocosm.

All beings, not just elementals, have a spark of spirit that connects them to the totality of the cosmos. Animist and pantheist perspectives would also say that all things that are manifest contain this quintessence. This spark is also the Rosetta stone, the translation key, that allows communication between beings from different orders of evolution and existence. Without this point of commonality, we would not be able to work with elementals nor for that matter many other types of nonphysical beings. By focusing your awareness on your higher self, your spark, you mesh with the place within you that has the capacity to understand the elementals.

The union of the Four Elements is what creates Ether, the Fifth Element. This synthesis of the Four Elements into Ether is part of the process of immanence, the upward stream of spiritual evolution that arises from the physical plane. Spirit is the downward stream from the transcendent planes that, comparable to the division of white light into the colors of the rainbow, separates and becomes the Four Elements. There is a lesson and a mystery about the Elements to be found by reflecting on the cycle of immanence and transcendence.

The diagram above can be used as a focal point for contemplation. It represents the Four Elements with the seed of the other Elements as spirals within small circles. In the center, there is a four-pointed star to represent Spirit and a circle with a four lobed figure to represent Ether. You may also wish to copy this figure and color it in with your preferred colors for the Elements.

I have often had students ask me why the elementals respond to our calls for their presence or assistance. Depending upon your background and beliefs, you may have a theological answer to this question. Some rely on the notion that humans have or can gain spiritual authority over lesser beings. That is not my belief, and I have an answer based on my understanding of metaphysics.

All things change and are in flux as long as they exist. Life swims against the current of entropy. There is a strong drive toward spiritual evolution in all beings. When beings observe each other or interact with each other, both are changed. When elementals engage with beings, such as humans, that have a fourfold nature, the part of them that is the seed pattern of the other Elements is enlivened. For example, given enough time and exposure to human energy, an elemental of Water may better grasp Fire, Air, and Earth.

Ritual work and magick involving the elemental spirits create opportunities for communication and energetic exchange. The process of communication between humans and elementals is mediated through the spiritual, divine spark within in each type of being. By connecting, directly or through resonance, through the functional equivalents of each other's higher selves, each party is given exposure to the other's vision of wholeness and unity.

For the elementals, this opens vistas onto a reality larger in scope than their own. With repeated contact with beings with the fourfold nature, the spark of spirit in the elementals begins to evolve. Please note that humans are not the only beings with the fourfold nature. Given enough time, elementals become more complex, more self-aware, and perhaps reach a tipping point where they cease to be elementals.

From the perspective of this line of reasoning, there is a strong potential for true reciprocity when elementals work with humans. The elementals are given access to experiences that would normally fall outside of the span of their reality. Thereby they can grow in wisdom and, perhaps with the turning of time, become more. The challenge for humans comes from the way the Elements within them are blended or woven together. To gain communion and use of their own elemental powers, humans need to experience them in a purer form to be able to separate and discern within themselves. Collaborating with elementals offers humans the examples needed to understand the Elements within themselves. When you ask for the elementals to support your work, they have very good reasons of their own to answer the call.

Beyond access to the powers of the Elements, one of the benefits that comes with proximity to elementals is a gradual refinement of your consciousness and self-awareness. Each Element has a distinctive mode of awareness, being, and presence. In humans, the four modes are blended—sometimes as summations, sometimes braided in multitasking, sometimes synthesized fully, and many other possibilities. When you can identify how the Elements within your psyche contribute to the formation of your consciousness, you become more fully awake and present.

There is also the possibility of becoming aware of the various processes that are normally unconscious. It reveals the metabolism of the psyche and the organelles of consciousness. Over time, this refinement can begin to expand the connection between your personal divine spark of spirit and larger fields of spiritual power. There is also the possibility of understanding the process of the synthesis of the Four Elements into Ether, which can result in powers that affect the physical world.

The coadunation of the Elements—the union of the dissimilar into a whole—results in the physical world. The Elements can express as forces, forms, essences, and as consciousness in the manifest universe. The Elements are a part of the substrate and the building blocks for the universe. As such, they exist throughout all of time and space in all planes of reality of the manifest universe. In a real sense, each of the Elements exists in continuous communion with every instance and iteration of itself throughout the vastness.

Every drop of water is connected to every other drop of water everywhere. The spirit in a candle flame is of the same spirit as the burning stars. If this is so, then the Elements act as a network that crosses through and joins different flavors of time from the linear to the eternal to the nonlocal. As such, connection to elemental consciousness may provide a back door into a grasp of states of time that are generally outside the default of human consciousness.

Elementals

The beings generally called elementals—the sylphs, salamanders, undines, and gnomes—vary greatly within their own categories. It is useful to compare them to physical animals and ecology to understand this. You would be right in asserting that mice and elephants are both mammals, but they are very different from each other in more than simply size. If we added great blue whales to the mix, the differences would be even greater.

The same may be said of sylphs or any of the other spirit beings who dwell in and are composed of one of the Four Elements. By extension to what is seen in the physical world, there should be the equivalent of everything from the elemental analogue of one-celled organisms to large intelligent beings to complex ecologies with myriad species in each Element. Think of each Element as being similar to a kingdom or domain of life or to a specific type of environment.

The spirit beings that we call sylphs, and so on, are just the ones that are of moderate size and whose self-awareness is within the range of human adaptability. The beings that are outside the area of your expectations are not targeted by your calls and invocations. It is hard to perceive or work with something unless you can hold it in your mind. In the case of nonphysical beings, this is even more important. Furthermore, unless you have modified your awareness to tune into beings that are out of the sweep of your normal state of being, your channel, you may not sense conscious beings, though you may still sense energies. This suggests that the elementals that respond to the names and invocations that are commonly in use are a miniscule sample of the categories, species, of elementals.

It is a mistake to think that elementals are lesser than humans because they do not have the fourfold nature. Many of them have been self-aware longer than human history and, as such, are our elders. Many of them are vast and contain more energy and essence than the most powerful human. Some of those that are individuated beings have deep wisdom and expertise in their specialties. No human being is a virtuoso in all fields of study or disciplines, so why should perfection be expected in other beings.

Elementals have their limitations, but so do all other beings. Assess each elemental as you would any other person's capabilities. The range of their intellect from the low end to the high end is broader than humanity's intellectual scope. Also, be cautious in projecting human emotions and personality structures onto elementals; it isn't a good fit and will result in misunderstandings.

Guardians

In quite a few traditions, it is customary to call for the presence of guardian spirits to watch over a ritual. When it is a system that creates sacred space using directional alignments, often these are beings that are associated with the Four Elements. The calling of the guardians of the watchtowers that is prevalent in many forms of paganism was inspired, borrowed, or adapted from Enochian magick and the Hermetic Order of the Golden Dawn.

It is said that these guardians are tasked with protecting against any harm coming from their assigned direction and from danger from their respective Element. When the elementals are explicitly named as guardians in the calls and invocations, those that embrace that role are more likely to respond. It is reasonable to assume that there are beings whose nature and temperament predisposes them to take on guardian or protective roles. It is also possible that some of the elementals that respond are not inherently guardians but take on the role in answering the request. It is of vital importance that you are clear in what is being requested of them in a protective role.

Calling in guardians may be exactly what is desired in some situations; conversely, it may reduce the amount of elemental energy available for use in the ritual for other purposes. The constraints of ritual format choices, and the limits of the physical plane and the planes closest to it, also serve to create a bottleneck, a bandwidth limitation for what and how much can be present. The capacities of the ritualists, and the place and time available, determine a portion of this as well. The point of contact with the physical plane and linear time that is created by your actions greatly determines what can manifest. A good question to ask when making choices about calling the elementals as guardians is whether that is their best role for the task at hand.

If the ritual or working has a focus on using or directing elemental energy, then it may be better to ward and guard the space in another manner. In this circumstance, I will call on the Elements in a more open-ended manner or with portals to their realms guarded by other beings. Another option is to call them as guardians and to do more ritual actions to explicitly ask for additional elementals to enter the ritual for other purposes. There is a ritual that we do in the Assembly of the Sacred Wheel wherein we open wide portals for the Elements in each direction with paths leading to a central altar that is presided over by a goddess who was been asked to offer blessings and protection.

Monarchs

You may have encountered mentions of the elemental kings in either witchcraft or ceremonial traditions. More often than not, when they are referenced, it is to give information on their place in a hierarchy or some tips on their invocation. Sometimes there will be a rambling discussion on the original source for information on the elemental kings and the derivation of their names. I have yet to encounter anything more definitive than gestures in the general direction of Éliphas Lévi, Paracelsus, and materials from the Golden Dawn. Despite lacking a clear origin story or provenance, I have found them to be responsive and useful in my rituals and workings.

I do not call them the elemental kings; I call them the elemental monarchs. The application of gender to the Elements is problematic and unnecessary. The identification of polarities such as positive to Fire and Air or negative to Water and Earth is descriptive of inherent qualities. The imposition of gender on the elemental monarchs creates unfounded associations and limitations derived from cultural expectations. My experience of them is that they are the summation of their Element. They are both individuated and hive minds that are the collective of each self-aware being within their Element. The names that have been passed down through the lore are Paralda for Air, Djin for Fire, Niksa for Water, and Ghob for Earth. The names are a miscellany with ambiguous beginnings and with an assortment of spellings in use, as well. Nonetheless, these names work when used to invoke the elemental monarchs.

The Monarchs themselves are older than any human naming conventions. They respond to these names as well as myriad other names. Their response to being invoked is more of a matter of the qualities present in the person calling them than the names used. Are the Elements awakened and harmonized within the caller? How much power has been raised and directed into the call? What intentions and outcomes are being held in the caller's consciousness as a coherent signal and a template for interaction?

That said, the names Paralda, Djin, Niksa, and Ghob have been in use for centuries and have built up a charge and a sturdy thought-form that are useful starting points. These elemental monarchs are my preferred recourse for calling higher order elementals because they contain a wide range of elemental beings and forces.

There are numerous other sets of beings comparable to the elemental monarchs in different systems of magick or traditions. Some of these have a greater emphasis on their Element, and others focus more on other qualities, such as their cardinal direction. When these are invoked, what appears is a mixture of qualities rather than a pure Element.

If you call upon the demonic Oriens, Amaymon, Paymon, and Egim, the results will be different than if you call upon the angelic Michael, Raphael, Gabriel, and Uriel. The Enochian names for the Elements from the Black Cross—Exarp, Hcoma, Nanta, and Bitom—are primarily composed of their respective Element, but calling them still shifts the focus to the worldview and planar geography of the Enochian system. Any of these may be the perfect choice for your practices, or they may add something that does not support your efforts. Examine your options and choose whatever is most harmonious and helpful for your goals.

Divine Beings

The definition for what comprises a goddess, a god, or a deity are fully dependent on the culture of origin, myths, teachings, and so on. As such, what may be considered a deity in one system may not be in another because the criteria are different. In many definitions or descriptions, there is a sense of vastness in size, perception, and power as a benchmark for being a deity. Even then, some systems rank them in orders of scale or on a continuum from divine to demi-divine to fully human.

I often use the terms "divine beings" or "great ones" to cover the territory of descriptions for deities across multiple systems. In addition to vastness, those beings that I characterize as being deities also have the fourfold nature, the three selves, and anything else required to make them a proper representation of the universe. Just as we are microcosms of the macrocosm that is the universe, so then are deities microcosms of the universe that is still at a much larger scale than the deities are.

There are goddesses, gods, and other kinds of divine beings that are identified as being of an Element, but I think this is misleading. There are tables of correspondences that list goddesses of Fire or gods of Earth, and so on, for every possible combination. Divine beings are more complex than one Element. It is closer to the truth to say that some divine beings have a special affinity for an Element or perhaps have been known to assist in working with an Element more frequently.

My natal sun is in Sagittarius which makes me a Fire sign, so I have greater access to Fire, but that does not mean that I lack the capacity to work with the rest. The Elements in divine beings can be thought of in a similar fashion. It is also vital that you do your own research on divine beings rather than trusting a listing of correspondences. What is listed as a god of Air may more accurately be represented as one of weather or specifically storms.

Divine beings with strong elemental connections have a strong influence or direct authority over the Elements or elementals. When humans have conscious awareness of the Elements within, they have access to their powers and a greater capacity to commune with elementals. Consider how much wider and deeper this would be for a divine being. Inviting the assistance of divine beings in working with the Elements is a request for the use of their talents, their insights, and their rank. Frequently, the request is for them to do the work one way or another. It may be a direct use of their own power, or through their power to convince elementals, to accomplish the task at hand. Though of a different order of magnitude, this hierarchical, intercessory approach with deities is similar to what happens when archangels or other formidable beings are called into play.

Attracting the attention and the favor of divine beings to do work with the Elements can be very effective. This is more likely to be the case if you have a strong working relationship with the deities in question. If you have not invested the effort to do so, then they are less likely to respond unless it also fulfills one of their agendas. It may be easier, and perhaps safer, to engage more directly with elementals or the elemental monarchs. When I do request assistance from deities on elemental matters, it is usually a request for guidance or communion so that I can better learn how to do it myself. Surprisingly, this does not seem to be a common practice.

The Elemental Realms

Where do the elementals live and where are their realms? I have heard a variety of answers to these questions, each of them bearing a partial truth suited to specific settings. For example, if someone is calling upon the Elements at the four directions in a ritual, it serves magickal and psychological needs to envision the gates as leading into a realm for each Element.

Years ago, I used to joke with friends about starting a pagan theme park that would include four elemental kingdoms that would put Disney to shame. These detailed imaginary realms are no more real than our descriptions for salamanders, undines, sylphs, and gnomes. Nevertheless, these images give human minds an interface that allows for methods to direct the power of the Elements. When it comes to magick, perception creates a functional reality.

My understanding is that these realms are not separate planes of reality nor are they equivalent to geography in any sense. These realms are more like channels, frequencies, data streams, domains, or multiplexed signals within each plane of reality. Like the wifi, cell signals, and other transmissions that fill the environment, the various realms go unnoticed until you tune in and decode them. When you are properly attuned, the elementals and their realms can be sensed as if you were wearing goggles that gave a heads-up display or an overlain augmented reality. However, the elemental realms only exist in the lower planes of reality. On the highest planes, the Elements are unified as Spirit and therefore are no longer separate entities or forces.

The elemental realms can also be thought of as states of consciousness. Each elemental experiences its realm as its home because their mode of consciousness is of one specific Element. As a result, their presence and awareness are limited to their frame of reference unless they are engaged with other beings of a different nature. The exchange of energy and information between various realms is strongest when self-aware beings encounter each other.

One of the other benefits that elementals gain from interaction with humans, or other fourfold beings, is the glimpses into other realms that they receive. There is a beautiful symmetry present in this because our glimpses into their realms can be a magnificent gift as well. Additionally, since perception reinforces existence, when beings perceive realms that are outside their normal range, they add to the vitality of that realm. When a person experiences one of the elemental realms, their thoughts and emotions feed it and also add to the storehouse of thought-forms associated with that realm.

5

The Sacred Regalia

The Tools of Magick

If you look at the imagery in the magician card in most tarot decks, you will find a chalice, a wand or staff, an athame or sword, and a pentacle or disc. You may have been taught that these represent the Elements and the four suits of the minor arcana in the tarot. That is true, but I'd like to place the emphasis on what these objects are used for—they are the tools of magick. More significantly, when you see a set of ritual objects that together represent the Elements, they can indicate knowledge and mastery of the use of their powers. The Magician has joined the knowledge of their internalized Elements with the externalized Elements; they have become the bridge between above and below.

Some refer to this set of ritual objects as magickal weapons. I choose to refer to them as magickal tools and, more exactly, as the sacred regalia. The word "athame," which specifically means ritual knife, will be used to mean "sword" as well, unless a distinction in usage needs to be made. Similarly, the word "wand" will be used to also imply "staff."

The term "regalia" in part references the objects and emblems such as crowns, scepters, ceremonial swords, jewels, and so on that are used in a coronation and that are passed down a royal line as heirlooms. The word "loom" used to mean tool, so calling these the tools of the heirs is right on the mark. Being on the path of magick, whether you call yourself a witch, magician, sorcerer, or whatever, calls for you to be a sovereign of your soul, invested with the powers of your divine nature, and prepared to take action in the pursuit of your life purposes. The sacred regalia for the Elements that will be described in this chapter are the athame (dagger), the wand, the chalice, and the pentacle.

I'd like to make a distinction between the sacred regalia that is a set of tools that symbolize the Elements and any of many kinds of enchanted or consecrated objects that can hold some of the powers of the Elements. For example, I have a metal bowl that has been consecrated and regularly used as a fire bowl, though at first glance you might assume it is a tool of Water. I have several wands that have been charged and prepared for a variety of purposes. I have been on this path for several decades, so I have gathered or created a large collection of ritual objects. I have one set that are my sacred regalia for the Elements that are the primary and foundational tools.

The pattern I use for the elemental tools is: the athame or sword anchors Air, the wand or staff anchors Fire, the chalice anchors Water, and the pentacle anchors Earth. The majority of magickal traditions that use these tools agree on the assignments for Water and Earth. The assignments for Fire and Air often vary from tradition to tradition, and the competing rationales for each are sometimes debated and discussed with the heat and the bluster of their sponsoring Elements. There is merit to assigning Air to an athame or a wand. The same is true for assigning Fire to an athame or a wand. The Elements existed long before humans were making objects. Though there may be coherent and aesthetic reasons for the elemental assignments, that does not make them inherent to the tools.

For me, Fire is closely connected to life force. The classic wooden wand or staff were once parts of a tree through which life flowed. The wand or staff also brings to mind the spine and the serpent-fire of life that coils about and runs through it.

It takes a wide range of skills and knowledge to create an athame or a sword. It seems fitting that the tool that requires the most use of the powers of mind in its creation is the bearer for Air.

When you work with a particular set of symbols, over time those symbols and their correlations become deeply embedded in your psyche. When that symbolism is made tangible in ritual objects, this process is swifter and has a broader impact. For that reason alone, I prefer not to assign the life force of Fire to the blade with all its martial implications.

In my personal mythology, my imaginings, I see my distant ancestors picking up a burning branch from a fire, and I see within that branch the ancestor of the wand of Fire. Far back in time, hands are cupped to drink water from a lake. Those hands later shape clay to reflect both lake and cupped hands in the making of a chalice. Thousands of years later, I see the powers of the mind creating the furnaces made hot by controlling air flow to smelt metal, to make forges, to make the blades of Air. I imagine a spiritual forerunner standing outside and turning in place, taking in the compass round of the horizon. Later they make a disc, a dish, a plate, an object that represents the world they stand upon. Over generations of practice, different symbols are inscribed on the disc in accordance with their traditions. The version I use today is the pentagram on a disc of wood. These are not sanctioned stories, they are personal imaginings, but these are exactly the sort of stories that deepen and enrich the inner connections to the sacred regalia.

The four tools of the Elements when laid before you on an altar are more than symbols; they are storehouses of power that can be drawn upon. They help to bridge the inner forms of the Elements with the universal Elements through their physicality and through the stirring of your imagination. The tools are a reminder that you are an heir to the powers of creation. The process of acquiring or creating your elemental tools along with their consecration and charging, is also the part of the process of awakening your powers. They are also meant to be used directly in your work. Though there are some similarities between the uses of the tools, each Element has distinctive benefits.

The Athame

The first use that comes to mind for an athame is the casting and calling of a circle or some other protocol for creating a container for magick and ritual. The power of Air is the power of the mind, and it is the mind that notices or imposes patterns and divisions. The consecrated and energized blade cuts and marks in the scribing of the circle and in writing symbols of power to open and close the gates. The setting, keeping, and sensing of boundaries is a part of the power of the athame. Many of the earliest symbols were cut, carved, and incised onto wood, bone, stone, and such. The energy of the history of making sacred marks with a sharp edge is inherited by every athame.

A cast circle, or any sacred space, that has been created with an athame may also be scanned with an athame. There is a resonance between the athame and the space that it has delineated. The athame is also a nexus point with the powers of Air that can sharpen your perception of any flaws or weak points in the circle. It can also reveal spiritual entities that are present, because their pattern stands out against the pattern you have created. The athame may be used as an antenna to extend your psychic senses. It may also be used like a dowsing rod to seek out specific things or to map the flows of energy in a place.

The athame is sensitive and responsive to veils and subtle energy. The athame can also be used to examine a person's aura to find breaches, weak spots, and irregularities. This can be done by holding the athame and feeling for tactile changes as it is aimed toward or brought near the person. It can be used as an antenna to draw in more energy to use other psychic senses to perceive the aura. To a limited degree, the athame can also be used as a tool for healing if what is required is the removal or the severing of a foreign energy pattern or attachment. It can also assist in work related to respiration or the resetting of the boundaries of the immune system. All of the elemental tools can be used for healing, though they each have specialties.

The athame, and expressly the sword, holds the power to protect and to banish. In a very direct fashion, the blade's energy can be extended to threaten or to cut. Ideally, circumstances will not warrant such a direct usage. The athame and sword can be used to scribe a boundary to protect or a boundary to contain and bind something unwholesome. When words of power are spoken, when words of dismissal are spoken, let the power of Air carry the words through the blade that they be heard crisply and strongly at every plane of being. The blade can also open gates and close them. Open a gate and let the wind of your words push out whatever needs to be banished, then close the gate.

The Wand

The wand carries the Fire of life force, and when you use a wand, it is an extension of your selfhood. This is one of the reasons that many traditions recommend that wands or staves be created from a measurement taken from your body. A common suggestion is that a wand be the same length as from the tip of the middle finger to the elbow—a cubit. Others suggest from wrist to elbow, and so on. The body's proportions follow the golden ratio, so any measurement derived from a unit of the body is resonant to the whole. While it is not necessary for a wand or a staff to match the proportions of its user, the custom of doing so reinforces the idea that these are very personal tools.

The wand can also be used to create sacred space, an energetic container, for spiritual and magickal work, but its properties differ from one cast by an athame. The energy that is directed by a wand or staff carries more of the imprint of its user than an athame, because it conducts both life force and will. Any changes to or pressures upon a wand-cast circle are felt more immediately and more keenly. Whether or not these properties are a benefit or a detriment depends upon the circumstance at play. It is also easier to add, subtract, or modify the qualities of sacred space on the fly when it is created with a wand.

The wand's affinity for the Fire of life makes it very useful in a broad array of healing practices. It can be used for dialing up or dialing down the chakras. The wand can be used to encourage the flow of energy through a disruption in the body, such as a wound or surgical site. It can also be used to draw energy into yourself to increase your vitality or to give you more energy to do healing work. If there is pain, inflammation, or a knot of stagnant energy, the wand can be used to draw that energy out and release it into the earth. Do not limit the curative uses of the wand to just people; it can be used for healing work on animals, plants, and even more generalized flows of energy such as damaged ley lines.

When it comes to working with spirits, a wand is generally less effective than an athame for protection or banishing. Wands are better than athames for calling spirits forth. Wands or staves can also be used to bolster your energy, your subtle bodies, so that you can remain more clearheaded in the presence of powerful spiritual entities. Sometimes, the difficulty in perceiving or understanding spirits arises from an overload of energy or overlapping energetic imprints. Wands and staves can moderate the excess and assist in sorting through your impressions.

They can also be used like ladders or yardsticks that allow you to move your center of awareness up and down through the ranges of frequencies and planes without getting lost or ungrounded. Remember that the wand or staff is also a representation of the spine and the chakra system. This capacity for attuning to different levels, frequencies, and planes also means that wands and staves can be used for rising on the planes. They can be used to facilitate astral travel, spirit flight, hedge riding, and other forms of journeying.

The Chalice

The chalice is underutilized as a tool for magick. The symbolic great rite of Wicca or the act of sharing cakes and ale in a ritual are important and sacred, but the chalice can be used for much more. A chalice can be used for scribing the boundary of a ritual by pouring out energy from the chalice while walking the edges of the space. An invoking pentacle can be traced in the air for opening the gates in much the way that you would with an athame or a wand. The sacred space that is created using a chalice is less secure than one cast by an athame or a wand. On the other hand, a fortress is not always needed nor desirable. The chalice creates a space that has more in common with a chapel, a woodland bower, or a dancing ground; it is inviting to both the seen and the unseen.

The Element of Water is reflective, mutable, attracts things to itself, holds them, and is a medium for energy and patterns; as such, the chalice is also an excellent vessel for skrying work. Gazing into your chalice helps to open the psychic senses to see visions. If it is a chalice that you have consecrated as one of your sacred regalia, it shares in the synergy of your vital powers. Water carries spiritual currents and is the medium for life. As such, it can be used as a vessel to act as an anchor for spiritual entities for communication. It is used by many for working with the dead and the ancestors, but it is not limited to those categories. For example, as a medium for life, the chalice can be used in healing ceremonies.

The chalice can serve as a portal to the astral plane. It can be used as a vessel in which you create astral forms, thought forms, that can then be released and sent forth as part of a working. The chalice has numerous uses in rituals. For example, it can be placed on an altar and be used in the same way that a statue or an icon can be used as a focal point for a deity or other divine being. To do so, you speak and direct your invocation to the chalice Additionally, it can act as the focal point for the raising of a cone of power. Used as a focal point, it can be a substitute for a practitioner that would otherwise be shaping the power. It is especially valuable when you are doing solo work and need one more set of hands or, alternatively, in a complex setting that already has all the practitioners occupied.

There are several practices involving the chalice that seem to be distinct and separate but arise from the same properties in that they are expressions of the same powers of water. Water holds onto energy, patterns, and intentions. It is also a conduit and portal for spiritual entities. The chalice, and similar regalia, can be used for offering libations. Chalices are often used in rituals of unification, such as a shared cup in hand-fastings and marriage ceremonies. Chalices can be used in sacramental rituals to join with deities, ancestors, or other types of beings. They can also be used for sealing solemn oaths and vows of any sort, because the Element of Water remembers, opens a portal, and carries the spiritual current.

The Pentacle

The pentacle can take the form of a pendant, a ring, an inscribed disc placed upon an altar, as well as many other forms, and it can be made of a wide range of materials. One of my favorite altar pentacles is a clay platter with a five-pointed star circled by a leafy border.

The distinction between the terms "pentagram" and "pentacle" have gotten muddled over the years, in part due to Gerald Gardner's writings. They have become mostly interchangeable in public discourse. When I was first taught about witchcraft, the word "pentagram" was applied to the drawn figure of a five-pointed star; physical objects, such as jewelry, were called "pentacles." This was a useful distinction.

Additionally, there has been quibbling over whether a circle around the star is what made it a pentacle and which of variant meanings for these words in mathematics, different traditions, and so on held more merit. There are also numerous ritual objects and charms called pentacles that feature a broad range of other geometric figures and glyphs beyond the five-pointed star. In this book, when I refer to a pentacle, it is a ritual object or ritual construct that has a unicursal five-pointed star as its main feature.

As the emblem of the Element of Earth, pentacles are used to represent protection, stability, and the structure of physical reality. These uses are a logical result of Earth being the Element of density and pattern, which is the essence of shape and boundaries. Pentacles also express the concept that the physical plane that we inhabit contains Air, Fire, Water, Earth, and Spirit as the Fifth Element. The five points of the pentacle also echo the shape of the human body—two arms, two legs, and the head—and, as such, are a reminder that we are a microcosm that reflects the macrocosm.

It should be noted that the pentacle does not contain all the Elements; instead, it encompasses the relationships between them and their internal structure. The pentacle is not the summation of the Elements, but it does have the instructions for doing the math. This aspect is why the altar pentacle can also be used to anchor power in a working or ritual.

In many protocols for creating sacred space, an athame or a wand scribes the air with energy in the shape of a five-pointed star, a pentagram or pentacle depending upon your naming preferences. This ritual action is done to open or close the way between the earth plane and other planes of being. That which can create or fortify a boundary or barrier can also do the opposite. The pentacle is also a diagram of elemental relationships, so it can also act as a map or a compass for opening to the desired realm.

Since the pentacle is the tool for Earth, and we live on the earth plane, its tool can also be used in lieu of an athame or a wand. I have been in numerous rituals where a pentacle has been used to scribe the opening and the closing of gates. It takes a bit more effort to move energy through a pentacle than it does an athame or wand, but the portals and gates that are produced are more durable.

The pentacle can be applied as a tool for healing, personal development, and integration. A significant measure of healing and growth comes from putting things into balanced relationships with one another and in their proper proportions. As an example, Feri and Reclaiming practices use a number of ritual constructs, such as the Pentacle of Iron, for these purposes. I used an altar pentacle on a person's abdomen as a focal point during a healing ritual. I have scribed an invoking pentacle onto a person, large enough to enclose their whole body, to call forth their self in health and balance. Take some time to imagine how you would modify these to fit your mode of practice.

The Tools of Ether

The Fifth Element—also known as Ether, Aether, Quintessence, or Spirit—is the actual summation of Fire, Water, Air, and Earth to produce something that becomes more than that sum. It is not uncommon for people to omit a specific tool for Ether in their sacred regalia for the Elements. Sometimes the representation for Ether is implied by the combination of items on an altar or conflated with images or statues for divine beings or ritual actions, such as acknowledgment of the above and the below.

These oblique or conceptual allusions to Ether are valuable but do not allow for a direct use of the powers of Ether. Moreover, a tool for Ether cannot be used well or fully unless the person using the tool has developed their capacity to work with the Four Elements.

I use either a cauldron or an egg made from quartz or obsidian as the tool for Ether in most settings. Although there is flexibility in how these tools can be used, I tend to use the cauldron for synthesis, creation, and opening to the void from which the manifest emerges. I tend to use the egg to hold, focus, or shape power. Both the cauldron and the egg can be used as emblems for the cycle of life, death, rebirth, and work related to the cycle of immanence and transcendence.

This is more about my psychological response to the physical shapes of these tools than what is inherently true. Nonetheless, emotional, aesthetic, or psychological responses have a strong bearing on magickal efficacy. More will be said about the uses of the tools for Ether in the chapter devoted to the Fifth Element.

6

Uses and Applications

Uses for the Elements

Perhaps the greatest difficulty in putting the Elements to practical use in magick or rituals is in the conversion of abstract concepts about the Elements for specific purposes. Often this results in blunt-force or simplistic approaches or in the avoidance of using the Elements at all. Since most practical magick revolves around having an impact on human concerns and mundane matters, the first step is to think about the Element as a part of human nature.

The next section of this chapter will give examples of hands-on applications for the Elements. In these instances, the Elements are used primarily as templates and as magnets to shape and to attract the desired outcomes. Then we'll explore uses for the Elements as power sources for your work.

The creation of each moment and each outcome in the manifest world is an ongoing process. The power of creation surrounds us at all times. Magick, among other things, is the shaping of that ongoing process toward chosen outcomes. The Elements have qualities and properties that we can name and understand, because we are aware of how they exist within ourselves. When we wish to shape the flow of creation to make magick, the templates, scaffolding, molds, and the organizing principles inherent in the Elements can be activated to speed and refine the process.

Rain droplets form readily when there is a tiny particle of dust or pollen that acts as a core that encourages the water vapor to become a drop. A miniscule fragment of a crystal of salt dropped into a supersaturated solution of salt will trigger the building of crystals. The presence of a focused nexus of an elemental energy pattern in a ritual or working will pull the resources needed out of the flow of magick and organize those resources to match its pattern.

When you are brainstorming possible ways to use the Elements, it is helpful to create groupings to help you to organize your thoughts. As an example, I will be listing uses for each Element within the categories of mind, body, and spirit. You could also devise uses based on categories such as the twelve houses or the planets, or the astrological signs, the ten spheres of the tree of life, the enneagram, as sub-Elements, et cetera. The broad outlines of almost any coherent method for classification can act as a framework for dreaming up uses. After reading about the applications I have listed below, you may wish to add to them or to create another list using a different system.

Mind

Air can be used for:
- assistance in studying or learning any topic
- finding the words for difficult and important personal dialogues
- releasing negative thoughts or mental obstacles
- being well spoken for court cases or job interviews, and so on
- finding new perspectives for problem solving
- awakening creativity and its expression
- understanding complicated systems
- the capacity to multitask better
- finding focus and calm in the storm of life

Body

Air can be used for:

- improving all things related to breathing
- a better singing or speaking voice
- planning and researching ways to create wellness
- quieting the mind to allow for proper sleep
- consecrating healing herbs, oils, and such for respiratory problems
- cooling down an overheated body
- improving hearing
- encouraging flexibility and ease of motion
- easing headaches

Spirit

Air can be used for:

- opening your psychic senses
- communicating with nonphysical beings
- assistance in divination
- inspiration and guidance
- opening or closing portals and gates
- help with astral travel
- greater clarity in meditation
- releasing attachments
- calling the power of hope

FIRE

Mind

Fire can be used for:

- increasing motivation for a task
- helping to bring about a choice or a decision
- the gift of charisma and personal power

- bolstering courage
- quelling fear
- pushing through an obstacle in your thoughts
- tightening mental focus
- transforming your perspectives
- intuiting strategies for battles of any sort

Body

Fire can be used for:
- summoning sexual drives and libido
- increasing physical vitality
- fighting infections and illness
- increasing warmth and circulation in the body
- providing stamina and endurance
- counteracting weak digestion
- encouraging the release of toxins
- strengthening muscles
- balancing the fight, flight, or freeze reaction

Spirit

Fire can be used for:
- banishing unwanted spirits
- cleansing away unwholesome energies
- setting a beacon to attract what you need
- growing your magickal power
- calling upon your higher self
- communing with divine beings
- seeking your life purpose(s)
- seeking insights into the mysteries
- understanding your true will

WATER

Mind

Water can be used for:

- releasing long-held feelings
- improving your self-image
- increasing your openness to new possibilities
- healing a broken heart
- mending relationships
- improving your capacity to read another person's state of being
- nurturing yourself and others
- refining your capacity to appreciate and create harmony
- finding a balance between the conscious and the unconscious

Body

Water can be used for:

- releasing stress in the body
- regulating sleep cycles, hormonal cycles, etc.
- bringing fluids in the body to balance
- improving balance and grace of motion
- better absorption of nutrients
- toning down allergic responses
- removing toxins from the body
- assisting in healing work that you do for others
- developing flexibility and easing joints

Spirit

Water can be used for:

- Past life recall
- dream work
- mediumship, channeling, and divine embodiment
- being a psychopomp or death doula

- ancestral work
- weather magick
- all the receptive gifts
- going into trance
- forgiveness and spiritual evolution

EARTH

Mind

Earth can be used for:

- better memory
- stable and orderly thoughts
- pragmatic and practical attitude
- unflappable and consistent determination
- encouraging proper psychological boundaries
- the power of discretion and discernment
- experiencing gratitude and satiation
- more patience
- more sensuality

Body

Earth can be used for:

- regaining strength after illness
- promoting fertility
- attracting employment and abundance
- finding a good place to live
- longevity
- strong skin, bones, and teeth
- better awareness of your body
- gut-feeling intuition
- better appetite

Spirit

Earth can be used for:

- creating durable shields and wards
- working with nature spirits
- enchanting plants to grow
- healthy connection with the lower self
- productive shadow work
- sealing or binding magick
- removing unwanted power by earthing it
- manifesting what is needed
- calling upon the web that connects all things

Elements, Purposes, and Nuanced Uses

The 108 suggestions for using the Elements listed above focus on using one Element for a specific task or application. These suggestions are also, for the most part, focused on using each Element in its constructive or default mode. More often than not, single Element solutions are seen as functioning by adding or focusing more of the given Element. However, the reverse can also be true, and the power of an Element can be used to reduce or dissipate its influence in a particular circumstance. Like does call to like, and an Element rules over itself. If someone is ungrounded or flighty, it may be that there is too much Air present, and asking the powers of Air to remove the excess is a reasonable approach.

Many practitioners choose to time their work with the phases of the moon to take advantage of the waxing and waning energetic tides. Sometimes a spell or ritual to increase something is needed during the waning moon, which is more suited to decreasing things. In that situation, the working must make creative use of what is available, like a sailing ship tacking back and forth to go upwind. Creative thinking is needed to find all the options available from each Element.

When determining what change you would like to promote, consider all the ways that the Element most related to the situation can be used. Do you need more or less of it? Is it a matter of concentrating or diffusing it? Is it about action or inaction? There are many other possible questions and perspectives.

Sometimes, you fight Fire with Fire. Other times, it may be more reasonable or practical to douse it with Water, blow it out with Air, or smother it with Earth. One of the other widespread tactics in elemental magick is the use of an Element as a counterbalance to cause the desired change or correction. Depending upon your background and training you may have some pairings that you think of as a natural counterbalance, such as Fire and Water. I recommend that you start with the idea that there is no default opposite Element and that each Element may be moderated by the other three. The important question to ask yourself is which of the other three redirects the flow toward the direction of your desired outcome.

There are some problems that are best addressed by two, three, or four Elements—all in the right proportions. After all, the physical world consists of all four Elements. However, it is easier to develop proficiency and understanding in elemental magick by starting with one Element, then a pair, and so on. Do not fall into the trap of thinking that if you cover all the bases by including all the Elements, you'll make up for any errors in your rationale or method.

In chapter 9, we'll be exploring the sub-Elements, which are Elements within Elements. For example, the Element of Water contains within itself the Water of Water, Air of Water, Fire of Water, and Earth of Water. Some really fine distinctions and adjustments can be made when you work with the sub-Elements. To make use of the precise and nuanced elemental magick of the sub-Elements, you must first be well vesed in working with the Elements as unities and as combinations of those unities.

Let's say that you are creating a charm to help you tell some difficult truths to someone you care about. You may wish to work with Water if you need more compassion. You may work with Fire if you need the strength of will to follow through. You may work with Earth if you are feeling wobbly or ungrounded. Or you may work with Air to help you find the words to do so. After you gain more experience, you may choose the Air of Water for this state of affairs.

Attracting and Directing Elemental Power

The first step in calling upon the power of the Elements for any purpose is to find and awaken the Elements within yourself. Your life experience and the material presented thus far in this book have given you an ample collection of ideas, images, and methods to draw upon for inspiration.

To begin, pick two or three of the colors, symbols, glyphs, or physical characteristics of a single Element. Do more than visualization, realize them in your mind, make them real with as many sensory modes as you can. Cycle through the two or three elemental foci at a moderate pace, letting them loop in your mind for a minute or two.

Then find the places in your physical or subtle body where you feel a stirring of power. Those are the places where some of your elemental power is present. Shift your awareness to the middle of your chest, gut, or wherever you feel your center of power to be. With each breath, let the elemental power be drawn to your center. When you can feel that enough power has gathered within yourself, you can take the next step. It will be a matter of experimentation to know what this feels like. The process can be sped up if you have someone who is psychically sensitive to monitor you.

Then begin to draw in more elemental power from the environment around you. Use the concentration of power in your center to act as a magnet, a tuned antenna, a nucleus, a central sun, to attract more of the Element that you are seeking. When you are holding as much as you can without crossing the line into real discomfort, you are ready to proceed with your work.

It takes power to raise, to shape, and to control power, so the first step was to gather enough to be effective with less overall effort. You can skip this step, but it just means that you may end up working harder to summon, cajole, push, and pull the energy of the Elements. Regardless of whether you are manipulating the energy directly or asking for elemental beings to assist you, having a focal point of elemental energy makes it easier to do the work. Elemental beings find it easier to perceive you and interact with you if they can *see* you.

A focused core of elemental energy can be reshaped to act as whatever tool you need. These thoughtform tools are more efficient, because they contain enough of the Element you are trying to affect to interact strongly with them. Perhaps this is because there is enough density of presence or overlap in frequency, plane of being, or phase to result in a firm engagement.

There are a variety of different courses of action that can be taken to work with elemental powers. The abundance of options can make it hard to decide upon the best action. I prefer a systematic approach to most things, so I developed four matching pairs of options for working with magickal power. This set of four pairs, eight options, is useful for thinking your way through the possibilities, even if you don't end up using one of these options. Power can be channeled or diverted, called or dismissed, embodied or abstracted, and focused or dispersed. For the sake of clarity, the term channeling employed here is about the flow of energy and is not related to its usage for spirit communication.

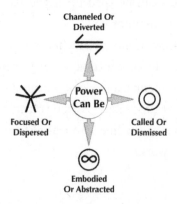

There is a loose affinity between these four methods and the Four Elements. The mode of "channeled or diverted" is associated with Water. The mode of "called or dismissed" is associated with Air. The mode of "embodied or abstracted" is associated with Earth. The mode of "focused or dispersed" is associated with Fire. Each of these methods can be applied to any of the Elements, though it is slightly easier to apply them to their respective Element. The four modes, eight ways, can also be used with other forms of magickal power, not just the Elements. I use the glyphs in the diagram as shorthand in writing notes for spells and rituals, as well as for visualizations to prepare for a working.

Channeled or Diverted

Channeling is perhaps the most instinctive method for manipulating energy, and thus is often the first method that is learned by most practitioners. The energy flows through you—your arms, hands, and so on—as if it were carried in your circulatory or nervous system. It is the mode used when a wand, or some other tool, becomes a tube or a conduit. Conversely, when we create a barrier to contain or exclude, then energy is diverted. A tube or conduit used in channeling energy also has walls, which are an example of diversion.

All the paired modes are linked and more like continua. Shields or wands can work through deflection and redirection, and this is an example of diversion being the primary mode. If you place a stone in a creek, it changes the flow of the water. You may have experienced the wind tunnel effect in cities where the buildings redirect the winds. Photographers use reflective surfaces to modify the available light. Spend some time remembering and imagining examples of channeled and/or diverted energy.

If you are filling, or charging, an amulet or tool with the energy of an Element, this is the quickest and most direct approach. This mode also gives a great degree of flexibility in controlling the quantity and the qualities of the energy. The reason for this is that the movement of the energy is often sensed directly in the practitioner's body. What you can sense can be managed with greater finesse. If more than one Element is being used, this mode makes it easier to switch and alternate between them. Creating a barrier around an amulet, a tool, a person, et cetera, that excludes or acts as baffles that slow interaction with an Element also falls into this category.

Called or Dismissed

In this mode, the power of an Element is called, summoned, beckoned to a particular time and location. This may be the calling of the energy of the Element or of a being such as an elemental, and it is a form of evocation. This mode relies upon the power of the mind and the imagination to assert that the chosen Element *will be* present in the desired location. It is the bending of reality with the power of a proclamation that the chosen Element's natural place to gather is the one you've chosen. It is the acknowledgment that power has built up, is abiding, and will continue to be in the time and place that you have called it to be. This may be within a crystal, in the center of a ritual space, at the tip of a wand, or any number of other options. If it is an entity, an elemental, then it is being charged with a duty to execute at a given time and place.

A dismissal is more than the ending or the reversal of a calling; a dismissal is also a powerful tool in and of itself. Whenever the problem to be solved is judged to be an overload of a particular Element, then a dismissal can be used to reduce or fully remove that excess. If it is inflammation with an excess of heat, then tell the unneeded Fire to depart. If the problem is swelling, then perhaps the Water should be asked to move on to another location or to return to its realm.

Sometimes, the surplus is not of a specific energy but of the presence of too many elemental spirits, resulting in a disturbed atmosphere in a place. In that situation, dismissals may be the method most suited to fully resolve the problem. The ability to perform an effective dismissal in some systems of magick comes from borrowed authority from more powerful beings such as deities. I tend to rely upon the influence that comes from self-confidence, persuasion, and established relationships. The single-mindedness that is used in summoning is also used in dismissing energies or entities.

You can also insert a calling or a dismissal into an object such as a magickal tool. If you have a temple room, an altar cloth, or a floor cloth used for ritual, you may also wish to embed a calling into these to aid your work. You can attach both a calling and a dismissal to an object, but if you do so, it is important that they remain independent and separate in your mind. Additionally, it is a good convention to have a key phrase, image, sound, et cetera that is distinct to control them.

Focused or Dispersed

Sunlight when focused through a magnifying glass, a convex lens, can turn warmth into a searing point that sets fire to paper. Sunlight passing through a concave lens, becomes cooler and dimmer. In this mode, it is through the power of your will that you cause the energy of an Element to become more intense and more concentrated. Depending upon the nature of the Element, this can be felt as greater heat, density, solidity, velocity, electricity, a spring-like rebound or push, and so on.

When you are focusing an Element, you are making use of the energy that is already in your immediate environment. Rather than channeling or calling in energy from elsewhere, you are harvesting and consolidating what is already present and converting it into a useful form or format.

It is important to keep in mind which of an Element's qualities you are focusing. It may be that you need all the qualities, or it may just be a subset of them that is needed. For example, it may be that what is needed is the light of fire but not its heat. To do this, you can apply your will toward only concentrating the light. This may work well enough most times, but even the best effort has a certain amount of bleed through, of blurring of boundaries. To continue with the example, if too much heat or other unwanted qualities are also accumulating, then it may be necessary to disperse them. It requires greater effort and attention on your part, but you can focus and disperse different qualities at the same time.

Dispersing, attenuating, or diffusing energy can be the best action to take if you need to quickly reduce the influence of an energy. Once the urgent need or distress is lessened by dispersing the energy, you can transition to dismissing or channeling away the energy, which takes longer to accomplish but offers a fuller resolution. When an entity is resistant to being banished, you can use as an alternative countermeasure the dispersion of the energies that it is using to manifest itself.

Embodied or Abstracted

It has been my experience that for most people this is the most difficult mode in which to achieve proficiency. To use this mode properly, you need to have a well-rounded understanding of the Elements and of how they exist and express themselves within you. This mode can be the most powerful of the four modes, but many are discouraged when they attempt it, as the results are small at first. Honestly, for most people, the growth curve for improvement is slow until there is a breakthrough. However, once there is a breakthrough, the improvements are steady. One of the barriers to overcome is whatever resistance you may have to thinking of yourself as a living, incarnate elemental being.

When you embody an Element, you have access to its powers in much the same way as you have access to your personal energy, your senses, and your physical capabilities. This is reminiscent of drawing down, aspecting, and divine possession, but it is more about awakening what is already present within you and connecting it to the flow of power around you, rather than acting as a vessel for something other than yourself. Although there is some alteration in consciousness in this process, it is much less than in divine embodiment. There is a dramatic difference in the flow and the volume of elemental energy that is available and the grace and finesse with which it can be used.

It is advisable to develop your skill to embody an Element one at a time. Trying to do two or more Elements before succeeding with just one generally results in no progress. One of the potential side effects of embodying an Element is the risk of acquiring an excess of that Element. After every attempt to embody an Element, it is necessary to return yourself to your normal baseline and balance. Grounding, centering, and other comparable practices should be used after each session.

Alternatively, if you have objects that you are using as repositories for elemental energies or have tools, amulets, et cetera that need charging, you can use them to absorb whatever excess remains. If you do not attend to your elemental balance, you risk discomfort and illness that can take many forms.

I use the word "abstracted" for the obverse, the other face, of this mode of working the Elements because it has enough meanings and subtlety to cover most of the possibilities. Embodiment brings whatever you are summoning closer to the physical plane, whereas abstraction moves whatever you are summoning toward higher planes.

Also, the span of your consciousness that is your core moves downward during embodying an Element and upward when you are abstracting it. When you embody an Element, you have access to more of its power. When you abstract an Element, you have more access to its wisdom and understanding of its place in the universe. It is easier to communicate with elementals, especially the higher order beings, when you have abstracted it.

Abstraction in this context is an elevation of the parts of your being that are of a specific Element to higher planes and higher frequencies. Like embodiment, you begin with becoming focused and aware of the Element you have chosen within yourself. The next step is to rise on the planes, to raise the vibration of your consciousness so that it may travel but with a variation on how it is done.

Instead of building the body of light, focusing your awareness into a spark, exiting through your third eye or crown chakra, or any other methods for astral or spirit travel, you focus only upon the Element and ask for its origin. The goal is to find the tug, the pull, back to its origin, and allow your consciousness to follow it there. This is a journey to the pocket, the sub-plane within the higher planes, that pertains to the Element that you are working with.

Spellwork and Ritual Construction

There are countless candles, charms, spells, and rituals that rely upon the power of the Elements for their efficacy. These are easy to find online and in books, so I will not take up pages here to provide you with premade workings. What I will offer is a pattern that will make it easier to design your own or modify existing workings. There are seven questions; in answering them, you will have a good plan of action or will have refined an existing plan.

1. What is the desired outcome?

Being clear on what your intentions are for any given spell or working is a valuable part of the process of analyzing your situation. However, knowing your desired, tangible outcomes gives information that will have a more direct effect on your planning. It has been my experience that giving more weight to outcomes than intentions produces more results.

2. Which Element is most linked to the outcome?

Linked is a neutral word that holds many possibilities. The Element that is most linked to the desired outcome may be sympathetic to it or its opposite. To create, modify, or transform circumstances to produce the desired outcome, should the linkage be supportive, adversarial, moderating, et cetera? There may be more than one viable approach; in which case, the choice may hinge on which Element you find it is easier to work with.

3. How will you gather the power?

Several modes for accessing power were presented in this chapter, and you may choose to use one or more of these, but how exactly will you use them? Will you be chanting, dancing, visualizing, concentrating, speaking words of power, and so on? Planning means figuring out the details to implement the working. Does the approach you wish to use complement the type of linkage you've identified? If it does not, change it to match the linkage and the desired outcome.

4. How will the power be held and directed?

Frequently, all or most of the energy is gathered, temporarily stored, and sent forth with the physical and subtle bodies of the practitioner. This may or may not be the best option. Are there tools, crystals, pouches with herbs, candles, or other implements that could augment one or more of the energy management tasks? In the case of a spell or working that is anchored in a physical object, such as a candle, a jar, a pouch, et cetera, consider using other materials to assist in gathering and depositing the power. Also, think through how the anchor object will project or send for its influence when it is in use.

5. Engines of creation or soil of creation?

There are other mechanisms of action that lead to a successful magickal working, but I often categorize them as either arising from the engines of creation or the soil of creation. These terms are my shorthand for two common approaches. If your efforts create an energetic blueprint that can be given to the unseen artificers, guided by the laws of magick, then you are using the engines of creation. This is a standard arrangement that is used to set a pattern in the astral plane or Yesod to cause manifestation.

You can use the machinery of the universe, with you as the artificer, and do the shaping, assembly, and deployment yourself. Another approach is to shape the intentions and the desired outcomes into a polished and perfect seed that is planted in the soil of creation. There it is left to sprout, grow, and be shaped by the conditions to which it must adapt to thrive.

Both approaches have their merits and their problems. The engines are more likely to give you what you want in a reasonable time frame. The soil can give you better than you could have imagined or miss the mark or the timing completely. It is also possible to do a working that is a bit of both.

6. What should the duration, duty cycle, and endpoint be?

Is your working a one and done, or is it an ongoing effort? Some goals are best achieved using a strong magickal effort followed by a timely mundane follow-up. Others are best accomplished using small, incremental gains and repetition. This determines whether you will need to do multiple energy raisings and workings. Is your design one that lends itself to ease in recharging or repetition?

If it is a tool, amulet, talisman, or charm, what serves as its repository for the elemental energies and patterns? Does it match the duration or duty cycle of its use? You may need to adjust your plan, because not all materials hold up as well as others. When the spell has done its work, or an enchanted object is no longer needed, how will you drain the remaining energy and decommission the working? Unwanted outcomes are more likely when you do not have a clear ending for a working.

7. How will you rebalance, give thanks, and make real offerings?

As your desired outcomes develop, and especially when they've been realized, make sure that you offer thanks to the Elements. This is a continuation of the process of releasing any excess energy and a good starting point for making sure that your Elements are in balance.

If it seems appropriate to the working that you've done, make some physical offerings. For example, pour a libation of water so that it may carry a blessing to the Element of Water. You could use a candle or a match for Fire. A sprinkle of soil would work for Earth. A deep breath blown into the wind for Air is a good offering. Remember, the Elements also learn and grow by contact with human energy and consciousness.

This chapter has offered a variety of perspectives, frameworks, and methods for using the power of the Elements. Some of you may be excited by the prospect of having new ways to think about spells, workings, and rituals using the Elements. Others may feel daunted by too many options and too many layers of information. I can tell you that what at first feels complicated becomes an easy flow of actions with repetition.

Once you've internalized these ideas and practices, quick and simple magick becomes more effective not just more elaborate. For example, I will often call the power of Air into my lungs before I speak to a large group. I also focus the Fire in my muscles before lifting something heavy. This takes little time and no planning, because I know these methods well. The best responses for any given situation fall somewhere on the continuum of simple to elaborate. It is good to be able to enact the full range of possibilities. Neither simple nor elaborate is better, it is a matter of what is right for the circumstances.

7

Contemplation and Personal Work

Air Moves Us

Air moves us
Fire transforms us
Water shapes us
Earth heals us
And the balance of the wheel
Goes round and round
And the balance of the wheel goes round.
—Cathleen Shell, Cybele, Moonsea, Prune

This chant appears on Reclaiming's "Chants: Ritual Music" album; it is available as a CD and streams on Spotify, YouTube, and other sites. I have loved this chant since I first listened to it on a cassette in 1987. Chanting it also led me to deepen my connection to the Elements and to find a way to understand myself more fully. It is a short chant, but it contains a great deal of wisdom. Let's look at its meaning piece by piece.

Air is the Element associated with thought, consciousness, and inspiration. Many of the actions that you undertake begin with a thought, an observation, a conversation, or an insight. Air is often the starting point, and its wind brings you the awareness of the out-side world and pushes you onward. So-called thoughtless action is a misnomer; it may be unconsidered or unplanned, but something was perceived in the mind that triggered action. Air does indeed move us.

Fire is the Element associated passion, will, and purpose. Once in motion, you experience friction and blow on the embers to call forth flames. Fire changes you through desire, the will to take action, and the burning away of distraction. Fire can purify or enflame, and it changes as it alters what it touches. Your life and your personhood are reshaped by the drive, the impetus, that Fire provides. Fire does transform us.

Water is the Element associated with the emotions, the subconscious, and all matters of the heart. You have feelings about your thoughts. You have feelings about your passions. Each minute of life's meaning is weighed against the contents of your heart. The shape of your life is carved by the rushing waters of the heart. The significance you ascribe to the people, places, and things are more about what you feel than what you think or desire. Water does shape us.

Earth is the Element associated with all that lives and the patterns of life. It is nature in all its forms from the smallest to the largest. It is the wisdom of instinct and of myriad carefully coordinated processes that maintain your body without your conscious attention. Earth is our plane of residence, the passage of time, and both womb and tomb. It is what restores you as you sleep and reweaves and rebuilds your body. Earth does heal us.

The Elements do not exist in isolation; they are forever turning in cycles of interaction that maintain the manifest world. Each Element is the beginning and the ending of a process. The Elements also interact with one another in pairs, triads, and as spokes around the hub of spirit in addition to the flow around the wheel. The critical thing to note is that health and vitality are dependent upon motion and interaction. The momentum shifts through each of the Elements. The balance of the wheel does go around.

I have used this chant to examine circumstances in my life to better understand my responses and motivations, both good and bad. By placing things into this fourfold system, you can gain perspective and find hidden connections. The process is simple and straightforward. Pick a situation in your life, not a nebulous issue but something that has specific details. The truth is more readily found in the details than in summaries or judgments. Then sort and filter those details through the Elements.

Starting with Air, inspect your thoughts, conversations, and your perceptions of the situation. Become aware of how these have moved you to take specific actions or feel particular ways. How would changing the framing, language, thoughts, or emphasis in your observations change your impetus and choices in this situation? Who or what is served by thinking this way? Decide if and how you will adjust or fully change your thinking on the matter.

Now focus on the Fire aspect. Let yourself become aware of the passions that have been stirred up by the situation. What appetites, urges, drives, zeal, longings, outbursts, and desires are moving around and through you like flames? Who do you become when you are enflamed by the situation? How are you being changed, transformed, by exposure to these passions? What is the proper level of intensity in your response to the situation? The goal is to find the right balance of qualities and intensity of engagement so that you are focused and motivated but not consumed or distorted.

The next step is a consideration of the matters of the heart and the domain of Water. Emotions reflect the circumstances with varying degrees of clarity and fidelity. The Element of Water can have things dissolved into it, can carry debris, and can be heated or cooled. Similar things can be said about the mixture of emotions in the human psyche. All feelings are real, but reality is changeable. What makes up the container for the circumstances you are in? What changes can you make to that container that then reshape your watery emotions? Do you need stillness to reflect or a fast flow to flush things out?

The Earth comes last in this sequence and will have the longest-lasting effect. When the thoughts, passion, and emotion have completed their cycles of action, what will remain? Can you work with these outcomes? Growth and healing, both physical and spiritual, require action followed by rest, recuperation, and reassembling. Once things have firmed up, there is an adjustment period. Have you given yourself the time and space to allow for this? Another possibility is that the things that are in motion will come to different completion points depending upon which resources are available. Are the materials, money, or other tangible assets present to reach the outcomes you want? You have a certain amount of choice in how you allocate what you have in the moment and in continuing efforts.

You may find it useful to complete one run through the Four Elements, allow some time for deliberation, then do it again. Write down notes or sketch or doodle a record for each repetition. When you have come to clarity, make a plan for how you will proceed to make the changes that are best for you. Eventually, you may find yourself analyzing your daily events on the fly from the perspective of the Elements. This is a wonderful development, but please make time to sit and do the more formal approach periodically. The best results for improving your quality of life generally come from a mixture of spontaneous and planned contemplation.

This chant does not contain all the possibilities for the elemental processes within a human. It does give an easy point of entry into thinking about how to do personal reflection with the Elements. If you know any chants, songs, poems, et cetera that have an Elements theme, you may wish to review them as possible source material for contemplation. You may wish to try your hand at writing your own. Don't be intimidated by the act of writing; it only has to meet *your* needs, not those of a publisher or critic. In my book *Casting Sacred Space: The Core of All Magickal Work,* there is a chapter in which I describe a ritual practice called the Four Minds that may interest you as well.

Setting aside the pattern of the chant that was used as an example, you can have productive meditations on the Elements in any sequence.

You may have a particular order that has been taught to you and is a well-worn path. It is useful to have a deep-seated pattern, and it is also good to know when to take a tangent. When you wish to consider an issue or situation in your life, pick the Element that is the most pertinent and use it as a starting point in the cycle. If you have the time and the interest, use each Element as a starting point for a set of cycles.

You can also home in on pairs of Elements that seem to be the bump in the wheel that is giving you a rough ride. If it is a matter of the head and the heart, then alternate back and forth between Air and Water. Explore the ways that an alteration in your understanding of your thoughts affects your emotions. See if a change in how you accept and process your emotions changes your thinking. If that does not fully resolve your challenges with balancing the head and heart, then work on adjusting the other pair of Elements.

In this case, it would be Earth and Fire. Look at the real-world circumstances and see what would make things better. Examine how you are using your money, time, and personal energy. What is your true will in this situation? What do you want? Are you fired up with enough motivation? Sometimes, the way to smooth the bump in the wheel is by increasing the rest of the wheel to make it match. At other times, the answer is to reduce the influence of the problematic Elements.

You can also examine challenges as triads of the Elements. (It is probably best that you have the experience of working with pairs of Elements first to get a sense of how to do this type of analysis.) Begin with the three Elements that you believe are out of harmony in a particular situation. Whether it is pairs or triads, don't assume that a specific set of Elements are always your weak spot. It is more likely to vary with different circumstances.

Then, after you have considered the three Elements that you have chosen—and hopefully written down some notes—swap out one of the Elements. Repeat the process of considering three Elements and swapping out one until you have done the four possibilities. Let's say you started with Air, Fire, and Water as your troublesome trio. Then you would work your way through Earth, Fire, and Water; Air, Earth, and Fire; Air, Fire, and Earth.

The process of swapping out one of the Elements and replacing it with the one you feel is stronger in that context often reveals details that you would otherwise not discover. If the goal is self-knowledge, growth, or the resolution of issues, then the finding of the unknown or overlooked is more helpful than the confirmation of what you currently think. Regardless of which method or approach you take in using the Elements, it is important to make space for what you don't know. One of the ways to encourage this is to systematically run through the possibilities and combinations. If you have a flash of guidance, follow it, but back it up by testing it.

If you use astrology or tarot in your practices, then there are more avenues to explore. Let's say you are looking at your birth chart, and you are reading it or having someone read it for you. After reflecting on the standard interpretations, pick out a few of your planets and meditate only on the Elements of their signs and what they mean for you. A good starting point might be your sun, moon, and any other planet that stands out. If you work your way through your chart using this method, you will find new information about yourself.

If you are looking at tarot cards spread out for a reading, you can add another layer of meaning by zooming in on the Elements they hold. The Elements are an essential part of the four suits of the minor arcana and are clearly assigned. Each of the major arcana cards also has an Element assigned to it, but this is less straightforward and varies depending on the deck and the systems of thought they are built upon.

For the major arcana cards, I sometimes use their assigned Element; while at other times, I look for a message in the imagery of the card as to which Element it holds in that reading. In addition to using the Elements as an adjunct for interpretation, you may also directly ask the question of what Elements need your attention to resolve the issues at hand. Pull a few cards with that question in mind as a way to select pairs and triads to explore.

Keep your mind open to finding messages from the Elements in any system of divination that you use. For that matter, look to small signs and omens in daily life. It may be that your eye lingers on the water from the tap as it fills the kettle. A flicker in a light bulb may be a message to pay attention to the Element of Fire. Did the wind change unexpectedly as you were speaking? The messages may not always be weighty and portentous, but paying attention sharpens your awareness of the Elements in your life.

8

The Elements and the Threefold Way

The Elements, and their fourfold nature, are present in the physical plane and the neighboring planes of existence. As you rise on the planes, the nature and expression of the Elements changes, and at some level they cease to be identifiable as separate. The higher planes are more expansive, higher in vibration, and less dense. The principles present in the higher planes extend to the lower planes.

There is an array of threefold principles, that originate in the high planes, that both surround and permeate the fourfold nature of the Elements. The threefold way expresses in a broader range of possibilities than the fourfold way of the Elements. Another distinction between them is the threefold powers have greater consistency of expression in different planes and forms, whereas the Elements transform more in relationship to their environment.

It is open to debate, but I think there are many more variations of the threefold principles than all the variations of the Elements. In philosophy, occultism, and religion, there are multiple expressions of threefold concepts, such as triune powers; trinities; the Hegelian dialectic of thesis, antithesis, and synthesis; the modalities in astrology; and so on. As such, I am selecting a just handful of these possibilities that relate more directly to working with the Elements.

Be aware that just as is true for the Elements, there are discrepancies in how different traditions or systems view the threefold powers. There is no one right way, and many routes reach the same destination. Even if you reach the same destination, and that is another question itself, the experience of that destination and whatever is the most salient will also vary.

The Three Modalities

If you have heard of or worked with the modalities, it is probably through the sacred science of astrology, where it is one of the fundamental building blocks. In the context of the Elements, modalities describe styles of representation and manifestation. The modalities exits above, below, and throughout the Elements.

The "cardinal modality" is the rushing energy that is the force of coming into being; it is pure impetus and desire, moving in a chosen direction. In its highest expression, it is the divine will to create. The "fixed modality" is the assembling and adjusting of energy to maintain homeostatic balance, a state of completion, and dynamic protection. In its highest expression, it is the divine will to preserve. The "mutable modality" is the energy of change; that is, flexibility, flux, death, and rebirth. In its highest expression, it is the divine will to evolve.

The Elements join, unite, and fuse to become one at the higher planes, as they follow the general principle of "as things rise, they converge." On lower planes, the Elements mix and combine but remain themselves and separate, though in new arrangements. The modalities remain themselves, with the same pattern of relationships, on every plane of reality where they exist. The Elements can interact with one another as pairs, triads, or as the full set of four. The modalities are either solo, or all three are present and interacting.

There is an affinity that exists between the modalities and three of the Elements. Fire is associated with the cardinal modality. Air is associated with the fixed modality. Water is associated with the mutable modality. This arrangement is taught in astrology and in the Western mysteries. It is important that this affinity not be misunderstood as a direct correlation or equivalency. It is reasonable to say that Fire is more at home in the cardinal modality. It is not accurate to say that the cardinal modality is more at home in Fire or contains more Fire.

In chapter 10 we'll be exploring Elements within Elements and the special relationship of Earth to the modalities will be clarified. All the Elements can behave in a way that exemplifies any of the modalities.

There are times when what you want to call forth for a working or ritual is an Element working primarily in a specific modality. Many years ago, I created symbols that I use to signify the modalities. I use these in my notes, I scribe them with energy in rituals, and I use them in visualizations. These symbols can be used to help focus your efforts to call for an Element with a modality emphasized. There is a simple visual logic to each of these symbols.

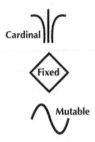

The cardinal symbol brings to mind a burst of energy. The fixed symbol combines the solidity of a square with the notion of balancing on a point. The mutable symbol is a segment of a sine wave moving from plus to zero to minus. I do not correlate any color to these symbols; instead, I use a color that matches how I am using them.

The Three Rays

The "three rays" are a subset of the "seven rays" family of concepts that is taught in Theosophy, and in some new age and Western mystery traditions. How the three rays and seven rays are taught varies in accordance with the metaphysics and religious teachings of each system that uses them.

One relatively common concept is that the seven rays divide into a group of three and a group of four. The first three rays are closer to the beginning, the source of the universe, and are more primal and more abstracted. The following four rays are closer to and more connected to denser planes of existence. In many systems, the four rays have intimations that they are mixtures of the preceding three.

Each of the rays guides, shapes, and manifests particular themes and universal tasks in a unique manner. Although each of the rays can be epitomized by the works of great teachers, divine beings, magickal currents, sacred writings, personality types, soul types, et cetera, there are no entities, incarnate beings, or spiritual beings that are the equivalent of elementals. All that exists may align with one or more of the rays, but they are not composed of the rays. It is an imperfect comparison, but think of the rays as fields of subtle energy and the Elements as fields of subtle and dense matter.

The first ray is power that arises from the might of will and the primal creative force. The first ray aims for and seeks freedom. The second ray is love that arises from the might of insight and intuition. The second ray aims for and seeks unity. The third ray is wisdom that arises from the might of mind and observation. The third ray aims for and seeks comprehension. You may find alternate attributions for the rays. Some prefer to refer to the first ray as will, the second ray as wisdom, and the third ray as active or creative intelligence. However, when you dig down into the descriptions of the qualities, to my way of thinking, it makes more sense to name them power, love, and wisdom.

Colors are associated with each ray. Although there are some connections, confusion will result if you try to match these colors to the ones for the sephiroth of the Qabala, the chakras, or the planets. The three rays are the primary colors—red, blue, and yellow—though which ray is given which color varies in different traditions.

If you decide to continue your studies of the seven rays, determine what color system is being used. In most, the three are the primary colors and the remaining four are secondary colors. Keep in mind how secondary colors are a mixture of primary colors to reveal how the three rays combine to produce rays four through seven. I use the assignments of red for the ray of power, blue for the ray of love, and yellow for the ray wisdom.

Each of the Elements represents each of the three rays in its own characteristic manner. When calling upon the Elements, you can include words, imagery, and intention that focus on the ray of power, love, or wisdom. By calling on the ray that suits your purposes, you fine-tune the form of the Element that manifests. The three rays can provide an overarching framework that helps produce outcomes more in line with your desires.

The first ray reinforces the power of will and the capacity to govern forces. The second ray reinforces the power to feel connection and the capacity to grow. The third ray reinforces the power to discern and to shape by cunning choices.

Christopher Penczak, in his book *The Three Rays of Witchcraft,* names them the straight line, the bent line, and the crooked line. If you have been intrigued by the three rays and wish to explore them from the perspective of a tradition of witchcraft, his book is an excellent resource. In the bibliography at the end of this book, there are other options to learn more about this topic.

The Many Threes

There are many threefold arrangements throughout magick, metaphysics, and religion. From the broadest and most inclusive perspective, all these arrangements, these schemata, can be seen as being linked. This does not mean that all these threefold patterns have straightforward correlations. The three rays and the modalities have wide applicability, but even with these, the context and framework of activity changes their relationship to other threefold patterns.

You may wish to study all these patterns, create charts or lists, and memorize what you can. I have done this and continue to do this with all things magickal. However, I also rely on my intuition and critical thinking to determine what fits when I am doing a working.

The Elements adapt and transform to become whatever is most suitable to the plane of existence, framework of activity, and collection of other powers that may be present in any circumstance. The Elements are like chameleons in that they change to match their environment while retaining their true shape. The Elements can and do match multiple threefold patterns at the same time. Since all these powers and patterns are multidimensional, the connections and correlations will shift depending upon the situation. There are an unlimited number of ways in which the fourfold and the threefold powers can combine. Bear this in mind when observing them, so that you might learn more, and when planning to use them in your spiritual and magickal practices.

The next section in this chapter is about threefold arrangements that differ from the rays or the modalities in important ways. They are more intertwined with one another, and the range of planes in which they operate is narrower. For each in this group of threefold arrangements, it is rare to see solo expressions of any of their attributes. In other words, they behave more like one thing acting as three rather than three things that diverged from a single point of origin.

The Elements of Being

I call energy, information, and essence the "elements of being," and this is a model I developed many years ago. I have described them several times in my writings. You can think of these as three channels that are present in everything that is manifest. Manifest does not just mean physical; it includes anything that has qualities that can be described.

In this context, energy is power and has attributes like frequency, temperature, color, speed, direction, and so on. Information is patterns and relationships and has attributes like language, concepts, names, formulas, flowcharts, causality, and so on. Essence is the hidden oneness and has attributes like synchronicity, infinity, mystic communion, eternal nature, and so on.

Although energy, information, and essence are present in every plane of existence, the relative proportion of each varies. In the lower planes, energy is predominant, followed by information and essence. In the higher planes, essence is predominant followed by information and energy. In the middle planes, information is chief, and essence and energy are roughly equal. This may be why the middle planes are used so frequently in magick.

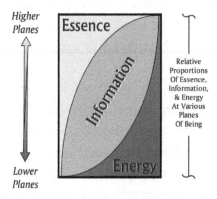

The Elements also follow this arrangement of proportions in the different planes of existence. In the lower planes, the Elements have a greater component of energy; at the higher planes, they have a greater component of essence. You may wish to reread and/or rethink some of the ideas presented in chapter 4, Spirits of the Elements. The nature, composition, temperament, and intelligence of elementals also tell you something about their native planes of residence when you consider their proportions for the three elements of being. Keeping this in mind will also make it easier to know in to which plane you should tune to find the types of elementals that you are seeking.

The Threes Selves

The lower self, middle self, and higher self are the three selves. Some traditions refer to this as the triple soul. You will find some variation of this threefold division of the psyche in the Anderson line of Feri witchcraft, some schools of psychology, the Western mystery traditions, Hawaiian Huna, several new age philosophies, Hermetic Qabala, and more.

My first exposure to the three selves was in studying Hermetic Qabala, where they are called the *Nephesh, Ruach,* and *Neshamah.* There is an affinity between the elements of being and the three selves. Energy is more closely aligned with the lower self. Information is more closely aligned with the middle self. Essence is more closely aligned with the higher self.

The lower, middle, and higher self can be thought of as body, mind, and spirit, but they are much more. The lower self is also animal instinct, the subconscious, the dreaming self, and our connection to the power of the Elements. The middle self is oriented to the flow of the physical world and waking consciousness. It speaks, sees, strives to understand, and grapples with what comes from above and below. The higher self is the portion of divine nature, eternity, and path of evolution that connects the universal to the individual.

When you call upon the Elements, you do so with three voices. These are the voices of your three selves, and each of these voices asks for the Element to appear in a different way. If you have brought your three selves into accord, the calls will be equally strong and offer the same message. This is uncommon, and it is more likely that one voice will be stronger, and there will be separate messages. This disparity can be a minor concern or very consequential.

If you become aware of your three selves before beginning an elemental working, you'll be able to engage the powers more fully. One of the simplest methods to do this is to focus your awareness—in sequence—on three locations in your body. Begin by moving your awareness, your sense of self, to your groin and become aware of your primal nature. Then move your awareness to the center of your torso and become aware of your thoughts and feelings. Lastly, move your awareness to the top of your head and seek the brilliance that connects you to all that is. After these three actions, proceed with whatever you have planned.

There are times when you want the power of the Elements to appear in a form that is more focused on one of the three selves. Perhaps what is needed is more primal; then the lower self would have the greatest affinity and skill to handle the matter. If the work involves managing, juggling, and adjusting things, then the middle self may be a better choice. Should the circumstances require guidance or spirit work, the higher self could be the best option. I suggest beginning again by moving your awareness to the three locations in sequence, but at each location, ask that specific self to cooperate with the plan to use one of the selves as the leader.

I have been asked a number of times about the connection between the three cauldrons and the three selves. The Three Cauldrons of Poesy—known as the cauldrons of warming, vocation, and wisdom—come from a 7th-century Irish poem. They sound like they should be related to the triple self or be a Celtic equivalent of a chakra system, but they are not. The cauldrons are broadly in this category but do not correlate directly to the three selves.

The cauldrons are more like an interface, energy constructs that are installed by meditative and magickal practice. The cauldrons are an allegory that when meditated upon, and worked with as an imaginal reality, lead to personal development. Once they are present and energized, they are tools to assist in opening to many blessings. The cauldrons on their own merit study, and I encourage you to do so, but they do interlock as well with the concepts of the Elements.

The Three Principles

The sacred science of alchemy works to produce practical and mystical results by working with physical materials and purifying and elevating their spiritual nature. The Elements are one of the foundations of alchemy; there are other fourfold patterns that are crucial, but there is also an important threefold pattern. That pattern is generally referred to as the *tria prima* or the three principles. The three are called salt, mercury, and sulphur. These names are not equivalent to their material counterparts. The Elements of the Wise are more than physical drops of water or sparks of fire. The three principles use the names salt, mercury, and sulphur as indicators and containers for larger ideas.

The Three Principles Of Alchemy

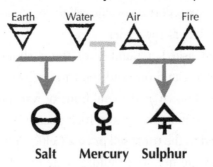

This threefold pattern differs from the rays and the modalities in that it is firmly anchored in the Elements. Moreover, the three principles do not express in all Four Elements the way the modalities and rays do. I view the three principles as a sort of incarnation of higher threefold essences into the denser forms of the Elements.

There are numerous interpretations and descriptions for the three principles in alchemy. Some of these portrayals are not in complete agreement, but rather than this being simply about different traditions' perspectives, it may be that they are viewing different levels of the three principles. Sulphur is seen as having the fiery qualities of the soul. Mercury is seen bridging the above and below as spirit. Salt is seen as the body, matter, and structure.

Sulphur is the union of the volatile Elements of Air and Fire. Salt is the union of the constant Elements of Earth and Water. Mercury is the union of Water and Air, which is mixture of the two. You'll note that the two positive polarity Elements make up sulphur. The two negative polarity Elements make up salt. Mercury is a mixture of the positive and the negative polarities, which speaks to its properties. For the purposes of this book, bear in mind that alchemical sulphur has an affinity with Ether and alchemical mercury has an affinity with Spirit. Salt has an affinity with all the physical expressions of the Elements.

The Three Worlds

The three worlds are a spiritual cosmological model, a way of mapping the shape, divisions, and conditions in different parts of the universe. This kind of model helps practitioners navigate to the other realms and figure out where they are within them. The most prevalent version of this model refers to them as the lower world, middle world, and upper world and is widely used in shamanic practices and soul-crafts for journeying.

Sometimes the lower world is referred to as the underworld, and the upper world is called the overworld or heaven. The lower world is the home for the dead—spirits of plants, animals, and primal beings. The middle world is the magical reality that is concealed in the world we live in and is filled with spirits and hidden folk of many kinds. The upper world is the home of deities, divine beings, elevated human souls, and ethereal spirits.

There are numerous threefold cosmologies and maps to the other realms. The Buddhist Trailokya, the three realms, is a map of the possible destinations for a soul between lives and/or as afterlife abodes. These three are known as K maloka, the world of desire; R paloka, the world or form; and Arūpaloka, the world of formlessness. A version of the lokas occurs in Hinduism and Jainism, with differences in theology but consistency in their having a theme of a realm for the underworld/primal, the earthlike, and the heavenly.

Another threefold map is that of the Celtic land, sky, and sea that has some similar associations. All these threefold world maps, and there are many more, are not the same. Each of these is distinct and serves the needs of its spiritual or religious community. The commonality that is useful in the context of the Elements is that the three-worlds model offers a useful portal of entry into altered states of being and a map for action.

The Three Worlds

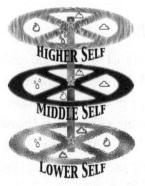

The Elements And The Selves
In Each World

I have a model that I find useful for working the three worlds and the Elements (see diagram). One of the keys to working with the Elements is to awaken them within yourself. To refine your awareness of the Elements within, meditate on how they appear in your lower self, middle self, and higher self. In this model, Spirt/Ether forms the axis that unites the three. You can visualize this as the central column of energy that aligns with your spine. If you prefer, you may see this as a tree instead. I have a friend who envisions an elevator for this process. One way or another, you move your center of consciousness down or up within this axis. The affinity that the three selves have with the three worlds is used to guide your awareness to each of the worlds.

The three worlds are mythic spaces, and they exist and are real in all ways that matter; however, many of the details of their appearance conform to what you believe them to be. You will probably have a useful experience entering this three worlds Elements process without setting the parameters of your mythic destination. If your goals are primarily self-exploration and self-knowledge, this will work well. However, should your goals be greater access and control of elemental powers, more will be accomplished if you enter with an established framework.

In the traditions I follow, Air is in the east, Fire in the south, Water in west, and Earth in the north. When I look for the Elements in the middle world, this is the default configuration I use.

I am an astrologer, so in the upper world, I see Fire in the east, Water in the south, Air in the west, and Earth in the north. This pattern is derived for the standard arrangements in charts. Also, in astrological charts, east and west are flipped so that east is on the left when facing north. In the upper world, the Elements opposite each other are in pairings of the same polarity. For example, Fire is the greater positive and Air is the lesser positive Element.

In the lower world, the Elements opposite each other are in pairings of opposite polarities of the same order of magnitude. Fire and Water are the greater Elements, while Air and Earth are the lesser Elements. In the lower world, Air is in the north, Fire is in the east, Earth in the south, and Water is in the west.

This is the process I normally use to work the Elements in the three worlds:

1. It begins in your core, your center. Close your eyes and move your center of awareness down to a place in your torso that is above the navel and below the sternum. This will vary from person to person, but it must be below the heart.

2. See yourself glowing, then shining, and becoming a brilliant star at your center. Become aware of the column of light that rises and descends from where you are. If you are already in the column of light, stay there for several breaths. If you need to, step into the column of light; do not rise or descend and remain there for several breaths.

3. Step out of the column and keep your eyes closed so as to focus on the hidden world. Giving yourself some time with each, look to each of the directions and become aware of how that Element appears there.

4. Repeat the sequence, but this time call out to the Elements and introduce yourself. Be patient and call out several times. If there is no response, bid farewell and say that you will return.

5. If you are no longer shining like a star, brighten up. Reenter the column of light and descend to the lower world. Once again, observe, then introduce yourself to the Elements.

6. Then rise and visit the upper world, using the same protocol. When you are done there, descend to the middle world but remain in the column of light. When you are ready, open your physical eyes. Let your center of consciousness return to whatever feels natural. Breathe slowly and orient yourself to the here and now.

It is a good idea to write down some notes on your experience. I use the colors, symbols, names, alignments, and so on to call the Elements that feel right to me. You may rework this three-worlds practice to match whatever you use. The only essentials are that you become a shining star, that you use the column to travel, and that you are respectful in dealing with the Elements.

The threefold ways are many, and there is much more to be studied than fits in a few pages. I suggest you tackle learning them one by one or in small sets. There are enough similarities between the various threefold systems that it is easy to get muddled unless each are learned well individually. These similarities are partly what makes them so useful in dealing with the Elements; the threefold systems exist in a broader universe than the fourfold systems. The threefold ways offer a framework large enough to create a container, a vessel, for even the largest elemental work.

9

The Platonic Solids

Almost every metaphysical shop that I've visited has sets of crystals for sale cut into the shape of the five Platonic solids. You will also find sets that include an additional two crystals, a sphere and a merkaba star, but these are not Platonic solids. These sets appeal to a broad audience, including magicians, pagans, new age people, lovers of sacred geometry, and mathematicians. These solids are also familiar to gamers who use dice with these shapes.

Cube

Ether/Spirit
Dodecahedron

Water
Icosahedron

Air
Octahedron

Fire
Tetrahedron

If you ask about the uses of the Platonic solids, the answers are often painfully vague. My experiences with the Platonic solids have convinced me that these shapes are resonant to the energies of their associated Element. This chapter will explore their uses, in addition to some background information about their origins and history.

Platonic solids are regular, convex, polyhedrons with specific geometric properties. They are three-dimensional forms whose sides consist of identical, regular polygons that meet in equal angles at the corners. These five are the only regular convex polyhedra. They are named after the Athenian philosopher Plato, who proposed that these shapes described the nature of the Elements at their smallest unit of existence. The Pythagoreans also studied them and provided Plato with his source material. The Pythagoreans are often said to have discovered them, which is a foolish notion. These primal shapes have been carved or depicted by many ancient cultures and occur in nature in minerals and living things.

Fire is associated with the tetrahedron, which has four triangular faces. Earth is associated with the cube (hexahedron), which has six square faces. Air is associated with the octahedron, which has eight triangular faces. Water is associated with the icosahedron, which has twenty triangular faces. Ether is associated with the dodecahedron, which has twelve pentagonal faces. The cube (hexahedron) and the octahedron are dual to each other. The icosahedron and the dodecahedron are dual to each other. The tetrahedron is dual to itself.

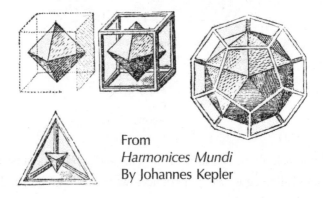

From
Harmonices Mundi
By Johannes Kepler

Being dual to each other means that the center of each face is the vertex of its partner. This relationship between the dual pairs is reciprocal. For example, you can derive the octahedron from a cube or a cube from an octahedron. There are many patterns of relationships between the Elements, and these, as illustrated by Johannes Kepler, are but one set. The tetrahedron is dual to itself, which reinforces the idea of Fire being the first Element to manifest.

The Platonic solids have captured the imagination of scientists, artists, philosophers, and magicians for generations. There are carved stone representations of the Platonic solids at the Ashmolean Museum in Oxford that are at least 4,000 years old. Mathematicians and scientists are quick to point out that Plato and Kepler were wrong in trying to apply the Platonic solids to answering questions about the physical universe and that their mystical conclusions are baseless. Devotees of sacred geometry and the mysteries are quick to overextend the overlap and the reach of the meanings and correlations that they make in both matters of science and spirituality. Regardless of your field of endeavor, it is best to think of the Platonic solids as an attempt to give shapes, characteristics, and names to units of existence that are numinous and eternal.

Kepler found that the Platonic solids were not a literal answer to explain the orbits of the planets; however, contemplating them led him to creating Kepler's laws of planetary motion. He was also led to insights on the music of the spheres and astrological harmonics that advanced astrology.

Robert James Moon, who was involved in the Manhattan Project, built one of the first cyclotrons, and built the first scanning electron microscopes, was inspired by the Platonic solids. He used the Platonic solids as a guide for understanding the nucleus in atoms. Moon also theorized that neutrons and protons are positioned in space at the vertices of nested spinning platonic solids.

The point is that the Platonic solids are meant to be taken figuratively as source material for insights and creativity. There are rare occasions when they are examples of literal truths, but the majority of their value is in revealing hidden symmetries and connections.

Uses for Platonic Solids Sets

Although much can be done with the mind, there is great value to using physical tools to make the work easier. You can carry more with a wheelbarrow than with your hands. Having physical representations means that you do not need to hold the shapes crisply in your mind while trying to multitask work with the Elements.

If you are attracted to working with the crystals, the sets made from various minerals also have the added benefit of storing a charge and an imprint. I have created models of the Platonic solids using dowel sticks or bamboo skewers that I have cut then glued together and have gotten good results. Online, you can find diagrams that you can print, cut out, and fold to make paper models of the Platonic solids.

If you purchase a Platonic solids crystal set, I suggest that you cleanse them of any energies that may linger upon them. Treat them as you would any other magickal tools. You have no way of knowing the circumstances of their creation or how many people have handled them or those people's states of mind when they touched them.

Use whatever is your preferred method for purification. If you don't have a favorite method, at the very least clear them by pushing energy through them until it feels like there is no resistance. One easy method is to take a quick deep breath while holding a crystal then as you exhale, slowly push energy down your arm and out the crystal. Please cleanse one crystal at a time.

Anchors for Contemplation

The first way that I used the Platonic solids as a tool for magick was in the form of a cut-crystal set. I used them to awaken a more tangible awareness of the Elements within myself. Visualizing colors, symbols, tools, or physical representations of the Elements is useful and a good practice. Holding something in your hand stimulates different parts of the mind and helps to link your inner and outer worlds.

When you grip a crystal tetrahedron in your hand or trace its shape with your finger while imagining the qualities of Fire, several things are occurring. You are feeding the tetrahedron energy, which, in turn, is transforming it into Fire energy as it resonates within the shape. You then begin to feel Fire from the tetrahedron, which sets up a feedback loop that allows you to produce energy that matches the pattern of Fire more closely. There is also a reinforcement of the association that what is held in the mind is also externalized in the hand. This makes it easier to move and shape Fire energy.

As you have probably guessed, you can do this with each of the Platonic solids. As a beginning exercise, you may wish to work with just one Element a day. If you have enough time and energy, you can do each of the four or five in one session. For the dodecahedron, which is Ether/Spirit, you will probably get better results if you first work with the shapes representing the Four Elements before adding the Fifth to your exercises. If you continue to work with the same set of Platonic solid crystals, they will develop a lasting charge and imprint that will make them a more useful tool for contemplation and other workings. I encourage you to pay close attention to where and how the energies of the Elements stir within you as you work with each one.

Altar Pieces

Once you've worked with the Platonic solids as anchoring points for contemplation and energy exercises for a few weeks, they are ready to be used in other ways. It is a common practice to use emblems of the Elements on altars, both in ritual settings and in permanent altar setups.

Sometimes these altar pieces can be natural objects that suggest an Element, such as feathers or seashells, or tools, such as wands or pentacles. I have also seen figurines representing sylphs, salamanders, undines, and gnomes on altars. Platonic solid crystal sets that you have energized are a powerful way to call and to focus elemental power on altars.

I have prepared altars on which I have used open framework versions of the Platonic solids and placed things within them. For example, I constructed an octahedron from slender dowel sticks and glue. I placed a feather inside the octahedron on an altar, and then enacted a ritual to imbue the feather with the power to call winds. Even if they are not being used as vessels to concentrate energy for particular magickal work, the open framework versions of the Platonic solids allow you to visually layer multiple representations for the Elements.

Never underestimate the power of a visually and symbolically rich altar to enhance your rituals. In most tarot decks, the magician card has an altar laden with the tools for the Elements, as well emblems for Ether/Spirit and sometimes allusions to Hermetic laws. I have conducted effective workings using a small altar that I could walk around, containing my tools and my Platonic solids crystals.

Circle Casting

I often create sacred space, energetic containers for ritual, that use the model of the Elements and the four directions as their core. It is customary to use a wand or an athame for calling the powers of the Elements, but you can also use the Platonic solids for this purpose.

If you have Platonic solids crystals that you have charged and consecrated to their respective Element, place them on altars at the four directions. As you go around to each direction to open the gates, lift the crystal and use it as you would a wand or an athame. You can also experiment with using them to scribe invoking pentacles, elemental symbols, spirals, and similar symbols as a part of opening the gates. There are differences and benefits to taking this approach.

Since these shapes are resonant to the Elements, they directly add to the power and persuasiveness of whatever call you make to the Elements. When they are put down on their directional altar, the Platonic solids continue to attract and to anchor the Elements without your further input. That alone gives you a good reason to experiment with them. They are somewhat less effective at opening the gates as compared to using traditional magickal tools. You will need to push a bit harder, but it is not a difficult adjustment. Though this may just be an idiosyncratic thing on my part, I find that the elementals that are attracted when I use the crystals tend to have a higher intellect and are more communicative. This may be due to the crystals or because I hold my own consciousness differently.

In Amulets and Such

There are a wide range of charms, amulets, talismans, spell bags, root bags, and so on that use the Elements as sources of power or as templates to shape the nature of the influences they provide. Frequently, the Elements are attached to these workings by roots, stones, oils, herbs, slips of paper with symbols, coins, or other physical anchors. These objects are selected because they are correlated with specific expressions of the Elemental forces. I am not suggesting that you dispense with using these materials in your work. I am suggesting that you consider adding Platonic solids crystals to your list of potential components. They will amplify and lengthen the life of whatever you create.

Platonic solids are available in an assortment of sizes, from very small to big enough to be the centerpiece of a shrine. The small ones can easily be added to bag, pouch, or sachet charms. As an example, consider adding an icosahedron (Water) to a charm for soothing a broken heart or for dealing with grief. In and of itself, the icosahedron won't make a charm for a broken heart, but will make the herbs, words, oils, et cetera that you put into such a charm more effective.

Look at what you currently do and brainstorm some possibilities. I created a wand from a copper tube that I filled with a full set of Platonic solids crystals, with herbs stuffed in between each as padding. One end was sealed with oak wood and the other end with holly wood. It is a remarkable wand for working with all the Elements.

Keep asking yourself how you would use a battery charged with an Element. Imagine how you would use a resonant chamber that amplifies an Element. How would you use a transceiver that facilitates communication with elementals? The potential uses for the Platonic solids reveal themselves the more closely you look at your existing practices.

10

Elements within Elements

The Sub-Elements

Earlier in this book, there were reflections and thoughts on how the Elements contain the imprint of the other Elements in order to function in relationship to the others in the manifest universe. This is also the how and the why of the Elements' capacity for growth and evolution when they engage with beings, like humans, that contain the fourfold nature. These nascent buds of the three other Elements within each Element are part of what is called forth when working with the sub-Elements.

However, that is not the whole story, as the universe is filled with echoes, repetitions, recursions, and leitmotifs. The Elements arise from a fourfold pattern, thus have an internalized fourfold pattern. So, for example, within Fire, there is the Fire of Fire, the Air of Fire, the Water of Fire, and the Earth of Fire. The same pattern follows for each of the Elements.

When we work with the Elements in most magickal or ritual operations, they are being called in their full form, which is the synthesis of their four sub-Elements. This is often the best choice, since it covers more of the possible needs for a working. There is also a power that comes from greater focus and selectivity. Calling the sub-Elements is a very effective way to dial in something very specific.

If you were planning to speak before a group to motivate them or inspire them, you may wish to charge a charm with the Air of Fire. This would be a good option if you want to impart clarity and passion to your words if you are a good speaker but not always charismatic. If you needed more help with your words and voice, with charisma as a secondary factor, then perhaps a charge of the Fire of Air would better.

A good way to learn and to understand the sub-Elements is to relabel them in terms of their correspondences and attributes. For example, the Fire sub-Elements could also be called the passion of will, mind of will, heart of will, and body of will. The Water sub-Elements could also be called the cycles of the heart, words of the heart, will of the heart, and touch of the heart. Write out as many versions as you can of the sub-Elements for each of the Elements. Periodically return to your list and add more as your knowledge broadens. You may wish to review some spells or rituals that you have done in the past to see how you would modify them to focus on a sub-Element based upon your list.

Do not limit your brainstorming of correspondences and attributes to those related to human nature. You may have encountered herbs, resins, oils, crystals, or other materials that have been tagged as associated with particular Elements. Often, different authors of traditions will have associations that do not sync up and conflict with each other. Some of the materials are capable of resonating strongly with more than one Element. Which Element comes to the forefront is a matter of what has been called.

Another option is to think of the possibilities of using the sub-Elements when using materials in working magick. Also think about how the sub-Elements express in nature and write down those insights, as well. I think of fog as resonant to the Air of Water, so when I wish to cast a spell to obscure something, I call upon the Air of Water. Over time, as you collect your observations and musings, you will create a treasury of sub-Element–based spell correspondences.

The sub-Elements are also used as descriptors and clarifiers in some esoteric systems. Among the fundamentals of astrology are the modalities and the Four Elements, as these give rise to the qualities of the twelve signs. The cardinal modality has an affinity with Fire. The fixed modality has an affinity with Air. The mutable modality has an affinity with Water. When you combine the modality and the Element of a sign, it yields its sub-Element.

As an example, Sagittarius is mutable Fire, which also indicates that it aligns with the Water of Fire. The affinity of the mutable modality with Water is what makes it the Water of Fire. Libra is cardinal Air, which makes it align with the Fire of Air. Applying this simple formula gives different insights into the qualities of the signs.

Sub-Elements Of The Signs	Fire	Earth	Air	Water
Cardinal △	♈ Aries Fire of Fire	♑ Capricorn Fire of Earth	♎ Libra Fire of Air	♋ Cancer Fire of Water
Fixed △	♌ Leo Air of Fire	♉ Taurus Air of Earth	♒ Aquarius Air of Air	♏ Scorpio Air of Water
Mutable ▽	♐ Sagittarius Water of Fire	♍ Virgo Water of Earth	♊ Gemini Water of Air	♓ Pisces Water of Water

Furthermore, the signs are also correlated to plants, crystals, et cetera, so thinking of the signs as their sub-Elements gives additional options for spellwork and such. The moon as it passes through the signs every month also emphasizes the sub-Element of each sign. The moon's sign, and thus sub-Element, also serves for timing magick for the best results. Please note that since there is no modality with an affinity to Earth, the sub-Elements of Earth are incomplete. This makes sense in that the zodiacal forces and influences are projected earthward.

There are a variety of tarot arrangements and systems, so of course there are also numerous ways to apply the Elements and the sub-Elements to the tarot. I'd like to point out before going further that there are many excellent tarot readers who do not apply correlations to Qabala, astrology, alchemy, or the sub-Elements to the cards. If you use the Coleman-Waite deck, or any of the many decks that adhere to its format, then these correlations are its foundations. I find the correlations to be useful, and they provide additional details and insights. I am sharing the arrangement that I use with no intention of suggesting that it is the best way. It is what works for my purposes. All divinatory systems have the potential to be used for operative magick. That which is receptive can be active, and that which is active can be receptive.

Following the same pattern as the sacred regalia, the suit of wands is Fire, the suit of swords is Air, the suit of cups is Water, and the suit of pentacles is Earth. This provides the overall pattern for the Elements in the minor arcana cards. The aces in each of the suits are the totality of their Element and as such can be thought of as the Ether or Spirit of their Element. By the way, the number of a minor arcana card identifies the sphere on the tree of the life to which it is connected. The names of the court cards can vary quite a bit from deck to deck, but the structure I use remains the same.

The four worlds of the Qabala inform the assignments for the court cards. Atziluth, the world of emanation, is associated with Fire. Briah, the world of creation, is associated with Water. Yetzirah, the world of formation, is associated with Air. Assiah, the world of matter, is associated with Earth. In the diagram below, you can see how combining the Elements of the worlds with the Elements of the sacred regalia produces the sixteen possible sub-Element combinations.

Sub-Elements of the Court Cards	**Wands △**	**Swords 🜁**	**Cups ▽**	**Pentacles 🜃**
King (*Knight*) Atziluth י	Fire of Fire	Fire of Air	Fire of Water	Fire of Earth
Queen (*Queen*) Briah ה	Water of Fire	Water of Air	Water of Water	Water of Earth
Knight (*Prince*) Yezirah ו	Air of Fire	Air of Air	Air of Water	Air of Earth
Page (*Princess*) Assiah ה	Earth of Fire	Earth of Air	Earth of Water	Earth of Earth

Tarot cards can be used as anchoring points or altar pieces when you do a sub-Element working. They are especially valuable if your task is Earth focused, because the sub-Elements for Earth are fully present, unlike the symbols available in the signs of the zodiac. The sixteen sub-Elements expressed in the court cards can also be thought of as personalities and styles of behavior. If the magick that you are doing is about augmenting or adjusting yourself so that you are better suited to a task or a situation, the court cards can serve as a template. Using all four of the court cards on an altar or at the four directions in creating sacred space can be helpful in calling on the spirit of an Element. If you add the ace card in the center of this configuration, it assists in contacting the monarch of its Element.

Using glyphs or sigils makes it easier to focus consciousness, intention, and energy, hence they are widely used in magick. They have great utility when placed on magickal objects, jewelry, et cetera to hold a specific pattern. Sigils are also quite practical when drawn on slips of paper for charms that involve using pouches, jars, bundles, and so on. Creating sub-Element glyphs using the triangle-based alchemical glyphs is easy.

You begin with a large version of the primary Element's glyph, then place a smaller version of the secondary glyph inside. I generally don't use colors with these, but that is an option if you want to do it. The sub-Element glyphs for Fire are shown in the diagram below. I suggest you work out the rest with pen and paper as an exercise to internalize this system.

Sub-Elements Using Alchemical Glyphs

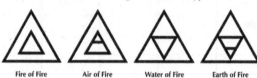

Fire of Fire   Air of Fire   Water of Fire   Earth of Fire

The tattva symbols for the Elements can also be arranged in a similar concentric pattern to produce glyphs for the sub-Elements. We use these in a variety of workings in the Assembly of the Sacred Wheel. Because the tattva symbols are not variations on a theme, like the triangles of the alchemical glyphs, it requires a bit more variation in size to place them within one another. I warn those of you who have a highly developed sense that things should be tidy to take a deep breath and relax. This variation in proportions and shapes supports some kinds of workings in a better way than the more regularized alchemical glyphs. As a reminder, the red triangle upright is Fire, the blue circle is Air, the silver crescent is Water, and the yellow/gold square is Earth. The diagram below shows the sub-Element glyphs for Earth using the tattvas.

Sub-Elements Using Tattva Glyphs

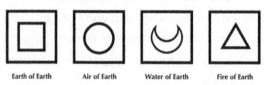

Earth of Earth   Air of Earth   Water of Earth   Fire of Earth

One of the benefits of the tattva sub-Element glyphs is that they have more differentiation, which makes them more quickly identifiable. When they are visualized, it is easier for all three selves to recognize the meaning and the qualities of a particular sub-Element. If the work to be done involves more inner work, visualization, or path-workings, I am more inclined to use these glyphs. It is also easier to fill this in with their associated colors and hold them in the mind's eye. Over the years, I have created flash cards, banners, and altar cloths using these, as they convey a lot in a simple visual code.

Patterns within Patterns

The sub-Elements arise from the fourfold pattern that created the Elements. The Elements came from a unity that divided into four parts, so each Element then divided itself into four parts as well. Elemental theory states that everything that is physical is made of the Four Elements in varying proportions. That is true, but a more detailed answer is that everything that is physical is composed of varying proportions of the sixteen sub-Elements. As your understanding of the Elements deepens and broadens, your appreciation for the sub-Elements and their application is likely to increase. I am sharing a ritual as the ending of this chapter to show you the sub-Elements as a basis for ritual.

A Sub-Elements Ritual

This is a ritual that I have offered at home, at conferences, and at pagan camping festivals that uses the sub-Elements of Water as its guiding principle. It is called the Chalice of the Four Waters ritual. You may use it as is, adapt it, or derive inspiration from it for your own rituals that use the sub-Elements. I generally hand out an outline to review and teach the ritual to a group before enacting it. In addition to the outline version, I have an annotated version for my own use and for teaching it to ritualists. In the version of the ritual included below, the annotations are in italics.

The desired outcome for this ritual is purification and healing through the Element of Water. Purification is often entangled with concepts of right and wrong or cleanliness and contamination. Another way of looking at purification is about removing those things that are not inherent. In this ritual, purification is about only keeping what is truly yours. The heart often hangs on to things that do not serve growth or learning.

Water is the Element known for both absorbing and for washing the emotions clean. Healing is a natural process that happens more readily when not encumbered by external influences that taint or tip the balance. The goddess Brigid is called upon in this ritual, as she is associated with the healing arts and sacred wells. I have a strong connection with her, but you may choose to call upon a different divine being, so long as they are compatible with the desired outcome.

Chalice of the Four Waters Ritual Outline

I. Crossing the Threshold

As you enter, look into a mirror, see your own eyes, and say:

"I open to purification and healing."

We continue to repeat this softly until all are standing in a circle or concentric circles.

Depending on the location and the numbers attending, there are adjustments that can be made. If it is allowed and desired, add saltwater and incense purification to this step. In certain venues, smoke or flame are not allowed, but where they are allowed, this is a good addition. Create an energetic boundary at the entry point before the ritual begins. Ideally, have one or two people holding the mirrors at the gate.

II. The Circle Is Scribed

Four people bearing chalices filled with water scribe and clear the circle. As they do so, we offer soft, freeform toning. The four people bearing the chalices take their places, each at one of the four directions.

Prior to the ritual, charge the water in each chalice with its sub-Element: Air of Water, Fire of Water, Water of Water, Earth of Water using words and perhaps a glyph. You may add a pinch of salt in each and cleansing herbs as an optional. The scribing is done by walking the perimeter of the space while envisioning energy overflowing from each chalice.

III. Invocation of Brigid

The goddess Brigid is invoked into this rite of cleansing and healing. Open your hearts to her presence. When asked to do so, repeat all or a few of these words with overlapping voices:

"She is here." — "She is!" — "Here she is." — "Here, here!"
When her presence is announced, say:
"Hail and welcome!"

The invocation should start as poetry, or at least poetic language, then become a brief visualization of seeing her appear in the ritual space. Ideally this is done by someone who loves Brigid and works with her. Use your voice and a visual signal, such as raising and dropping the arms, to close the repetition of the overlapped words. You may substitute another deity associated with healing if you like.

IV. Calling the Four Waters

The four directions are called in the form of the four Waters, using a chalice at each. We will offer a chant at each direction. Some possible chants to use are given at the end of the ritual. You may listen to them at my website, and they are also available on CDs and as MP3s.

You may use whatever water chants are thematically correct for your needs. After each Water is called, all say thrice:

"Here and Now, Within and Without!"

The brief calls should be focused on the sub-Elements of Water. They are Air of Water, Fire of Water, Water of Water, and Earth of Water. They should also include statements about and the healing of the mind (east), soul (south), heart (west), and the body (north). An invoking pentacle of Water is scribed at each direction using a chalice. The chants should be started and led by an appointed bard for the ritual or the chief herald, if that is possible. Another option is that the four people calling the directions may each start their own.

The sequence is calls, chant, "Here and Now . . ."The chants should each be done three to four times.The west chant should be done more slowly than the rest.

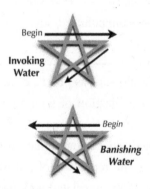

V. Accepting and Cleansing

Take a moment to become aware of something that you wish to accept, cleanse, change, or heal in your heart. The chalices will be taken from person to person around the circle. Dip your finger in the water of each chalice with your intention.

When all have touched the waters, the chalices are slowly poured into the cauldron/bowl on the central altar. All "aum" softly as this is done. When the last of the waters are poured, the toning becomes louder and peaks.

Offer words and instructions for people to dig deep and open up. If it is a small group, everyone will dip their fingers in all four chalices. If the group is larger, then each chalice will serve one quarter of the circle. If it is a large group, one drummer softly drumming to hold the space is useful.

Those bearing the four chalices should walk inwards in a spiral to the central altar, then pour the water slowly as all tone. Ideally, all four chalices will be empty at once.

If you have drumming, it should stop as the water is poured into the cauldron/bowl.

VI. The Spirit of Water

Offer words of welcome for the presence of the Spirit of Water. In groups of three to five, people go to the cauldron/bowl on the altar. They gaze into it for guidance and energy. They may dip their fingers in the water if they like. While this is happening, this chant is offered:

I Will Be Gentle with Myself
I Will Love Myself
I Am a Child of the Universe
Being Born Each Moment
—learned from the singing of Libana,
from their recording "Fire Within," *www.libana.com*

The chalice bearers take a few steps back to make room for the approach of people to the altar. Have a few people demonstrate this step to get things started. The chalice bearers and/or other ritualists continue to silently call forth the Spirit of Water to help maintain the power focused at the altar.

VII. Thanks and Closing

Words of blessing are offered, and we say thrice:

"We Give Thanks"

The four Waters are thanked and dismissed, and we end with:

> *The Circle Is Open but Unbroken.*
> *May the Love of the Old Ones*
> *Be Ever in Our Hearts.*
> *Merry Meet and Merry Part*
> *And Merry Meet Again.*

Thanks is given to the seen and unseen, the powers of Water, to Brigid, and all who chose to participate. Brief dismissals are given at each direction. Ideally, use the banishing water pentacle at each direction. The water in the cauldron/bowl should be taken outdoors and poured on the ground or into a body of water as an offering. If not immediately possible, please bottle up the water and do it later.

Chants

East (Air of Water)

"Waters of Life"

Water, Waters of Life
Gentle Rain, Soft Mist, and Tidal Pools
Hot Beating Blood, Cool Ocean Deeps
Water of Wonder, Mystery of Our Hearts
Water of Wonder, Mystery of Our Hearts

—Ivo Dominguez, Jr.

South (Fire of Water)

"Holy Well and Sacred Flame"

Holy Well and Sacred Flame
Maiden, Mother, and Crone
Bright One Be Here
Bright One Be Here

—Ivo Dominguez, Jr. (inspired by a Reclaiming chant)

West (Water of Water)

"Three Streams"

Blood of my blood
Stream of life—flow in me
Soul of my soul
Stream of love—flow in me
Spark of my spark
Stream of light—flow in me
Stream through eternity
Stream through eternity
Stream through eternity
Stream through eternity

—Ivo Dominguez, Jr.

North (Earth of Water)

"River of Eternity"

Tears of joy and tears of sorrow
Blood that beats and blood gone still
Down the river, down the river
River of the Ancient Ones

River of the yet to be
River of Eternity
—Ivo Dominguez, Jr.

Notes

To enact this ritual, you need a minimum of five people: four chalice bearers and one lead ritualist who provides instructions and cues.
Other tasks that can be assigned to these five or given to additional
ritualists are purification at the gate, chant leading, and drumming.

The physical objects needed for this ritual are one or two mirrors,
four chalices, a cauldron or bowl on a central altar, and (optionally)
saltwater and incense, a drum, and any other decorations or visual
elements that seem suitable. It is also a good idea to measure the volume of water needed to fill but not overflow the cauldron/bowl and
fill the chalices accordingly. Also, a hand towel hidden under the altar
is a good idea.

11

Fire

This is the first of four chapters that take a closer look at the Four Elements. These chapters will be a collection of observations, lore, and musings on the Elements. As such, the style of presentation will be more like vignettes and tapas that range from poetic imagery to magickal theory. They will hopefully inspire you to examine the Elements with your reason and imagination to develop your own view of their characteristics.

Heat and Light

Fire has both light and heat as attributes. Sometimes, light and heat are present in equal measure; at other times, they are fully separate or are present in varying degrees. We experience the fire of the sun as having both warmth and light. We see the light of the stars but do not feel their heat. Although this can be explained in terms of the science of the physical world, there are also metaphysical implications. The axiom of "as above so below," along with the doctrine of signatures, asks us to look deeply at how every plane of reality is in concordance with every other plane. Fire's properties vary in accordance with the laws and patterns of each plane.

The part of fire that behaves like light is of a higher frequency and of the higher planes. It is the least material and most expansive portion of fire and closest to the Spirit of Fire. The part of fire that behaves like heat is of a lower frequency and of the lower planes. Heat is fire of a denser sort, as its motion has become entangled with dense and subtle matter. The motion of fire moves back and forth in the vibration we experience as heat. The proportion of light and heat that is experienced is an indicator of both the nature of that particular fire and of whatever or whoever is interacting with the fire.

Portals

In one of my first lessons as a witch, I was taught that fire is a portal. The lights were dimmed in the room and before each of us in the class there was a lit candle. We were instructed to examine every part of the flame. After doing this for a time, we were to adjust our breathing to match the energy we felt. The brighter part of the flame could be used as a portal for skrying, seeing things from other times and places. The darker part of the flame close to the base and the wick could be used as a portal for traveling. This is one of the reasons that physical fire is used in so many rituals and workings.

Every spark, campfire, blazing star, eternal flame of the other planes, et cetera bears within it the fire that has existed throughout all of time and space. When you hold two candle flames close to one another, they are drawn to each other to become one flame. Fire has no fixed boundary of itself. When you have a flame before you, and you have placed yourself in synchrony and sympathy with its energy, you can connect with any time or place where fire exists. This is easier when you have a physical flame as a proxy for cosmic Fire, but you may also open the fiery portal with the Fire within.

Passion

One of Fire's primary correlations in the human psyche is passion. The correlations to willpower and life purpose are fairly straightforward by comparison. The question that is typically posed about passion is whether it falls more rightly in Water's domain. The emotions are assigned to Water, and the question hinges on whether passion is an emotion.

In magick and metaphysics, the definitions of common words take on new meanings to make up for the lack of proper terms. For the purpose of describing the Element of Fire, the passions move a person toward motion, toward action. The passions are the hot feelings—such as lust, the thrill of competition, desire for a person, place, or thing—that push to you do what is needed to fulfill that passion. Passion is usually felt strongly in the physical body, often affecting heart rate and breathing.

Passion can also be expressed in the pursuit of knowledge or inner experiences, as these are still motion and action, though more internalized. Fire's correlations of will power and purpose are what best moderates the passions. This will be clearer when you read the section on emotion in the Water chapter.

Three Fires

The three rays are woven throughout each of the Four Elements. When the three rays express themselves singly in an Element, they also reveal more about that Element. The ray of power when it shows itself in Fire takes the form of the electric Fire. This is the Fire that moves like electricity in a circuit. Electric Fire is driven by polarity; like an electric current, it arcs and jumps between gaps to reach its goal. It is a pure form of passion. When you feel the electricity of excitement coursing through you, it is Fire under the sponsorship of the ray of power.

The ray of love when it shows itself in Fire takes the form of the solar Fire. The sun warms and lights the world to make life possible. This is the Fire that enlivens all that lives and burns in your blood. It radiates to reach in all directions without the need of circuits or polarity.

The ray of wisdom when it shows itself in Fire takes the form of the need-Fire. This is Fire that is drawn out of matter by friction, by raw necessity, by the rubbing of wood to wood. This is the Fire that purifies and drives out distress. This is the force-fire, wildfire, witch-fire, and nauthiz that is also the Fire of evolution—both physical and spiritual.

If you call on Fire in one of the forms sponsored by the three rays, you will have access to these powers in a more concentrated, purer state. For example, Fire in its generalized form can be used for purification, but when it is called forth as the need-Fire of the ray of wisdom, it is stronger. Not only is it stronger, it is more discerning in knowing what to leave and what to remove. Perhaps more important than the increase in power that comes of calling the three rays is the greater intelligence of the Elements that manifest in accordance with the ray that is called.

Aries, Leo, Sagittarius

Even if you have little background or even interest in the sacred science of astrology, I think that you will find value in knowing more about the signs and their Elements. The focus here is on the pattern of the signs and the specific form of the Elements that they can call. You can conjure the signs by using their names; their glyphs have power as well. These are powerful templates for helping to shape the Elements in your magick.

The three Fire signs describe how selfhood and personality are shaped by Fire. Aries is cardinal fire, so it is the Fire of Fire. It holds the strongest drive and passion of the three. It is the primal force of bringing things into being and shows Fire's generative power. It also holds the quickest path toward defensive or destructive action. Leo is fixed fire, so it is the Air of Fire. It holds the greatest power of will and persuasion of the three. It is the Fire that is steady and eternal, that warms and lights all with equanimity. Sagittarius is mutable fire, so it is the Water of Fire. It holds the power of questing for your life purposes and their enactment. It is the Fire that can be just a glowing ember or a towering pillar or flame, as it is adaptable to what is needed.

Atziluth

In the broadest sense, the four worlds are the default system for the planes of reality in the Hermetic Qabala. However, this fourfold pattern repeats itself in different scales and scopes. So one could say that there are four worlds in each sphere or four worlds in each world, bringing the number to sixteen, and a score of other arrangements and numbers. There are myriad schools of thought on the proper arrangements for worlds, Elements, and so on. I will keep it to what I prefer and that which is most applicable in this setting. For now, especially if you are not a student of the tree of life, let's envision the four worlds as they relate to the Elements.

Ideas are realized into Thought. Thoughts are formed in Imagination. Imagination is expressed into Form.[1]

This is a remarkably succinct description of the four worlds, which are also known as the world of ideas, the world or realization, the world of formation, and the world of expression. The names of the worlds are Atziluth, Briah, Yetsirah, and Assiah, and, yes, the spellings vary from source to source. If we convert this to an elemental ordering it becomes Fire, Water, Air, and Earth. The ideas of Fire are made visible as thoughts reflected in Water. The thoughts in Water take on detail and greater reality in the imagination of Air. The detailed imaginings of Air are constructed into solid forms by Earth.

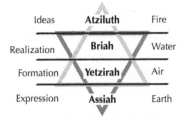

The Element of Fire is closest to its true nature when manifesting in Atziluth. This is the highest world, closest to the Source of all

---

1   Tim Keen, "The Four Planes of Manifestation," *Solomon* newsletter, *www.servantsofthelight.org*

things, and the absolute Atziluth is beyond our reach. However, there are many lower octaves, or analogues, of Atziluth in all the levels that we can reach while incarnate. When you seek Fire in the highest plane within your reach, you are also seeking your divine spark. That Fire that is your divine spark is also seeking communion with the eternal Fire on the road to the Source. This, too, is an example of the passion of Fire.

Sacred Fires

It is a good habit to put the same sort of thought and effort into the setting and the tending of fires for ritual purposes that you would grant to any other part of your practice. Whether it is the lighting of candles, charcoal for incense, or a bonfire, you are working with a delegate from the realm of Fire. If you do not recognize this, all is likely to go well enough, but it is a missed opportunity for a fuller engagement.

As a starting point, treat the physical fire with the regard that you would give a Fire elemental. If not that, then imagine it as an open window or gate through which the beings of Fire can see and hear your actions.

If you are anointing a candle, placing herbs or resins on charcoal, or feeding wood to a bonfire, think of these also as offerings or messages to Fire. It would be lovely if you added spoken words to that effect, but just changing your understanding of your actions changes the dynamic. This perspective may have an impact on what you think and do while scribing symbols or words onto candles that you use in workings.

When setting up a sacred fire in a fireplace or outdoors, I will often scribe symbols in the ashes or on the ground before placing the kindling and wood. If part of the ritual involves throwing herbs or other materials into the fire, speak to the material to carry the message. You may also wish to actively envision a portal in the flame.

When it is time to extinguish a sacred fire, take the same care that you would offer in closing down a ritual or casting. Words or actions that let the fire know that it is about to be extinguished allow the elementals in attendance to do whatever they need to do at their end. Offering gratitude and thanks are always a good idea for both the givers and the receivers.

A question that I have often fielded is whether it is better to snuff out or blow out a candle. Some practitioners have very strong feelings about this, especially if the candle was the focus of a working. I believe that it is a matter or energy management, intention, and the physical action, so there is no one right method.

Your breath is a conduit for your power, so if it used to blow out a candle, it can disrupt the work you've just accomplished. However, if that breath is used with intention and finesse, it may be additional energy that sends forth the work like wind in a ship's sails.

I often pinch out the flames with my fingers and use the brief heat and tactile sensation as a signal to seal the work and release it. However, if your fingers are tender and it takes several attempts or you burn yourself, you may be adding a disruptive energy of a different sort. If you use a snuffer for extinguishing candles, you must still consider the how and why of doing it. It is an action that can have an impact on your working, and using a snuffer does not remove these considerations. In each situation, think through what you are communicating, your intention, and what your energy is doing to choose your best method for extinguishing a fire.

12

Water

Cleansing and Transformation

All of the Elements can be used for cleansing, though Fire holds a special prominence. Water is the Element that we use on a daily basis for physical cleansing. Water also has a long history of being used for spiritual cleansing. Purification baths are a widespread practice for healing, the removal of negative workings, and as a preparation for important rituals. There are also rituals to wash the hands and feet for spiritual purposes. For example, spiritual healers may wish to cleanse their hands before and after performing a healing. There are floor washes to clear negative energy from a place or to call wholesome energy into a room where someone has been ill for an extended period.

One of the reasons water has so many uses is that it has the power to attract and to hold onto energies. Energy and matter can also be carried away, but water is selective in how and what it draws into itself. Through the use of prayers, spells, directed energy and/or the addition of salt, herbs, et cetera, the water is charged and petitioned to do specific work.

In the process of cleansing someone or something, the water becomes increasingly contaminated until it can no longer cleanse. Water, like all of the Elements in their highest forms, cannot be corrupted; however, a finite quantity of water can become fouled. This is truer for physical water more so than subtle water, or the elemental energy of Water, but once separated from the cosmic Water, any of these can be sullied. In nature, both physical and subtle, water renews and cleanses itself through cycles of transformation.

Water is often used in initiatory rites and rites of religious passage. While it is true that the use of water for a ritual that is a rebirth has a strong symbolic connection to the physical act of birth, there is more going on than that. Part of it is the action of the cleansing power of water. The Element of Water is also able to convey energetic changes and patterns to the person who is receiving the ritual. Water also has a strong connection to cycles of life and nature and as such can provide the current to encourage a new turn of a person's cycle.

Cycles

Water is always turning in various cycles in nature. Water in the oceans evaporates and rises to form clouds that in turn rain down. Some of the rain falls straight back into the ocean. Some of the water takes a longer journey home through rivers that eventually reach the ocean. Some rain goes deep within the earth where it can stay for days or millennia before rejoining the ocean. There are many other cycles and journeys that water is taking sequentially and simultaneously.

It is as if the water were incarnating in all these forms to learn all the possibilities. The currents and motions of all of water's cycles have momentum that acts as a sort of memory of those cycles. It is also through these cycles that individual portions of water become purified. Water is cleansed through distillation, filtration, and so on; it cannot cleanse itself without the transformative properties of cycles.

Portals

Water has a long history of acting as a portal to other times, places, realms, and realities. I have a vivid childhood memory of seeing a cluster of sky-blue puddles set in red Georgia clay in a friend's yard. The sky was cloudless and brilliant, and the angle of the sun was just right. For an instant that stretched out for an eternity, I completely believed that if I stepped into the puddles, I would be in the sky.

Humans have been seeing reflections and ripples in bodies of water in the landscape since their beginnings. Fog, rainbows, ice, and other forms of water in nature have also been perceived as portals and gates. For the sake of portability and convenience, the practice of using bowls and other vessels to take advantage this property became widespread in ancient times.

The Element of Water is a universal solvent; it dissolves all things, including the boundaries between times and places. Water's natural tendency is to descend and fill and touch every surface, every volume, every shape within manifest reality. Water's true color is the color of light, and it reflects, refracts, and transmits light. With these properties, water easily becomes a portal for the passage through or the perception of all that it touches. As a point of information, glass is technically a very viscous liquid that partakes of some of water's qualities; this is one of many reasons why glass and mirrors act as portals so easily.

Emotion

Water of the heart, of the emotions, is one of the first correlations that sticks in the memory, with images of tears of joy and sorrow. In the chapter on Fire, I began to make a distinction, for the purposes of understanding the Elements, between the passions and the emotions. The emotions of Water are inward responses to what begins as external experiences. Water takes the world and reflects it and takes it inward.

If I am on the bank of a lake, and I marvel at the beauty of the trees and the sky reflected in its still depths, I am having a Water emotion. If I then have the desire to have a cottage by the lake with a porch facing the water, I am having a Fire emotion. A simplistic approach, that is nonetheless a good start, is to consider the Water to hold the receptive emotions and Fire to hold the active passions.

Think for a moment of the words "pull" and "push" and whatever associations or images they bring up for you. Water is magnetic, it pulls at you and pulls the world in. Fire is expansive, it pushes you and pursues the world. When you walk, or engage in most kinds of motion, there is a coordinated interplay of muscles pushing and pulling to make it possible. It is the interplay of Water and Fire that forms the emotions and the passions. Water provides meaning, which is more lasting than the passions of Fire. It is in Water that the summation of the swirl of impressions and sentiments made over time is created. Water determines the value and significance of things in your life.

Three Waters

The ray of power when it shows itself in Water takes the form of the Water of shaping. Water also knows how to be solid, liquid, gas, and plasma. This is the Water that shapes the babe in the womb, that creates canyons and snowflakes. This is the Water that bends, refracts, and reflects light to reveal Fire. This is the Water that is the medium for waves of every sort and the revealer of fine structures.

The ray of love when it shows itself in Water takes the form of the Water of unity. Two drops in close proximity draw together to become one in unity. In Water, the power of surface tension is writ large, large enough to fold and hold the boundaries of cells and the edge of the universe. It is also the Water that finds the lowest place, fills the container of its circumstances, and creates a level surface.

The ray of wisdom when it shows itself in Water takes the form of the Water of memory. As Water touches and travels through all of time and space, much is dissolved into it or carried along in the current. Water remembers what it has touched, dissolved, or carried. It remembers everything that it has reflected, and takes the without and makes it within.

The powers of Water, when called through the sponsorship the three rays, give access to the deep processes that operate at a universal scale. These powers of shaping, unity, and wisdom are present in Water in all its forms, but by calling them as the rays, they are amplified and concentrated. These powers are of particular value in healing, performing operative magick, and matters of the heart and communities.

Cancer, Scorpio, Pisces

The three Water signs describe how selfhood and personality are shaped by Water. Cancer is cardinal water, so it is the Fire of Water. It is passion of Water to nurture all that it has birthed. It is Water acting as a parent to creation. It is Water eternally shaping the world to make a home for life. Cancer is the generative power of Water.

Scorpio is fixed water, so it is the Air of Water. Unlike Air, Water cannot be compressed, so any pressure applied is distributed equally throughout the medium. It knows, does not forget, and reaches every space and place. Scorpio is the Water that descends the deepest into matter and mind.

Pisces is mutable water, so it is the Water of Water. It is the Water that longs for connection and equanimity. It seeks to level all things and is universal unity. It is the power to become one with the shape of boundaries and containers. It is the ocean without a shore.

Briah

In the four worlds model of the Qabala, Briah is the world of realization and creation. The principal color correlations associated with spheres of the tree of life are called the Briatic colors. This is the level wherein the attributes that we can hold as thoughts in normal human consciousness become possible. This where the emanations of Fire in Atziluth, the unseen formless and eternal Fire, are made visible and intelligible by the power of Water in Briah. It is Water that makes light visible, thought possible, and the existence of forms an inevitable outcome. It is in Briah that the powers of Water to shape, to nurture, to dissolve, and to remember are at their strongest.

There is one Briah, yet it is also many. The four worlds exist as manifest realities; as imaginal, perceptive, and cognitive spaces; as microcosms and macrocosms of themselves; and more. The four worlds are like four musical notes, some that we can hear and some that rise or descend beyond our capacities. The Element of Water is present in every Briah, and all Water is one Water. Through the lesser waters that we can touch, it is possible to reach the iterations of Briah that are beyond our touch. This is one of the great utilities of the Element of Water in magick.

Sacred Waters

Water that has been consecrated or charged—that has been tasked to do work in a ritual, a healing, a blessing, as an offering, and so on—merits respect. When you prepare water with energy, words, and/or additions such as salt or herbs, be mindful that it may also be picking up on your unspoken thoughts and emotions.

If you are gathering water from rivers, oceans, rain, et cetera, please offer thanks for the loan of the water for your purposes. Elementals and other spirits will take note of your actions. When the ritual or working is finished, then the water should be returned to nature. If possible, I prefer to offer the water as a libation by pouring it into the ground or a body of water. If that is not an option, then I will pour the water into a sink. As I pour the water down the drain, I envision the water reaching the ocean or the soil. If the water is clean of physical or energetic contaminants, I may use it to water house plants. Think through what you have done with the water and come up with a way to release it that matches your intentions.

If you collect waters from sacred locations or that has a connection to a particular place, be mindful that over time that connection and energy will fade or become muddled. The longer it is away from its point of origin, the more it will absorb the local ambient energies.

Think of this fading the same way you would herbs or oils that you have in your magickal cabinet. Keeping them in a cool dark place is a start. Since what you are trying to preserve is the energy pattern in the water, ward your cabinet. As a secondary measure, I will ward and seal the jars and vials I use to give an added layer of isolation. When I do open the jars or vials for use, I remind the water where it came from and envision its origin. I reach out in my mind to the source of the water and its proxy in my hand.

13

Air

Cleansing and Adjusting

The burning of herb, resins, woods, et cetera to produce smoke and scent for cleansing, purification, or to facilitate magickal rituals is nearly a universal practice. When I first started on my path in magick, the name for this practice was suffumigation, and the action was called either censing or suffumigating. Over the years, people began to use the term smudging as a general replacement for these terms, even though smudging is both material and culture specific. I prefer to call it censing, in most cases.

Air is the Element most strongly associated with the mind, with words, with communication. Fire cleanses by energizing or heating things until the contamination is reduced to its constituent parts or to nothingness. Water cleanses by dissolving, absorbing, and removing the contamination. Air changes the pattern of the contamination or encourages it to depart.

When material is burned, its energy, or vibration, is released and becomes a message for whatever it touches. Each particle, each molecule, contains the message, and Air itself vibrates with the message. It may be a request or a command to depart. It may be the raising or changing of the spiritual atmosphere so that only certain patterns or energies can remain. Air can be very selective in what it invites or dissuades.

The cleansing power of air can also be accessed by using sound. This can be in the form of the human voice, bells, singing bowls, drums, or other instruments. Sound charged with purpose can cleanse, charge, promote healing, or change the qualities in an environment to match your intentions. I have a bell that I rely upon for quickly clearing a space, but in a pinch, banging a wooden spoon on a pot has done nearly as well.

Air conveys meaning and if applied with coherence and force, it attempts to impose the structures of that meaning. Air is the medium and the messenger, but the practitioner must deliver the message. Air's power to cleanse, call or dismiss, and modify the qualities of spaces makes it essential in many magickal operations.

Inspiration

Air is thought of as the lesser positive Element and as comparable to the lower octave of Fire. Fire is the first Element that emerges from the plenum of all possibilities and is closest to the Source. The primordial force of Spirit is tempered and cooled as it passes through Fire and Water so that when it is in Air, it can be held in consciousness, in human awareness.

The words "respiration," "inspiration," and "spirit" are linguistically linked, and that happy synchronicity also tells the tale of how Air connects them. Air is correlated to the powers of thought, imagination, and so on. What is often forgotten is that these powers, like Air, span a broad range of possibilities from the subconscious to the hyperconscious. Air allows for the creation of a shopping list and the inspiration for a new theory in physics or a new style of music.

Air is the medium and the muse but not the source of inspiration. Air is the principle of agency. Air sponsors an individual's decision-making and action, as well as communication and collective action. Air can move in continuous flows and in punctuated bursts, as it is both verbal and nonverbal consciousness. The creation of sigils, formulas, symbolic images, poetry, and similar densely rich constructs are Air arising. Sometimes, inspiration arrives in your awareness and needs to be unpacked, decompressed. Other times, the inspiration comes in the work of taking what you know and compressing it. Air can expand and contract but remains itself.

Openings and Transportation

When sacred space is delineated, when a container for magick is created, it is the Element of Air that is most at play. The words, the visualizations, the protocols, and so on that establish the space rely upon all the attributes of Air. Whereas Fire and Water in and of themselves form the material and the openings for portals and gates between times and places, Air provides the keys, locks, and hinges for these gates.

It is through the power of language, under the sponsorship of Air, that calls and invocations to spiritual entities are made. Sometimes the use of Air as an intermediary or liaison is direct and evident. I have been in rituals where the personifications of the four winds were called upon to open the ways and deliver messages to bring forth elementals, deities, et cetera. Air contains the magick of names and words of power.

Air is also about motion and transportation. It is the air, the wind, that is ridden when traveling in spirit form. The astral journey, the ride to the eternal sabbat, the descent to the underworld, and other voyages are facilitated by the power of Air. The association of wings and flight with messenger beings of various kinds, from archangels to deities such as Hermes, is significant. It is more than just the psychological symbology of flight; it is an indicator of their connection to Air.

Thoughts, Passions, and Emotions

It is Air, with images and words, that connects the passions of Fire with the emotions of Water. Air is the go-between, the push and pull, the hot and cold of externalized and internalized responses. Air is neutral, and pure mind finds the middle way between both ambivalence and strife.

Since you tend to identify strongly with the stream-of-consciousness voice of your mind, and Air carries within itself representations of the passions and the emotions, these are all braided and mixed in your self-awareness. This is one of the reasons why you can be overwhelmed by the swirl of Fire, Water, and Air in your mind. When those Elements mix and clash, storms can result.

Meditative and contemplative practices work in part by creating separation and awareness of the Elements within. Mind that is pure Air can know emotions and passions without creating a whirlwind. As things rise, they converge; so if the Air of higher mind is reached, then it is easier to achieve higher heart and higher will. The path of magickal and spiritual evolution relies heavily on working with the Element of Air.

Three Airs

The ray of power when it shows itself in Air takes the form of the Air of commanding. Air understands that all things are vibration, akin to sound both physical and subtle. To know a name for a thing is to know and utter its vibration. The closer to its full name the utterance, the more fully it responds. Vibrations can be amplified or canceled by combining sounds. The Air that commands can create, modify, or destroy by changing the patterns of vibration.

The ray of love when it shows itself in Air takes the form of the Air of mutuality. Air moves more freely than the other Elements; it can rise or fall and has no preferential direction. It is drawn to where there is a lack of Air. Where the pressure is low, Air rushes in from where it is high. Air conveys oxygen for red blood, carbon dioxide for growing plants, sounds for all beings that hear. It conveys the weather, scents, seeds, pollens, and more—equally to all and without boundary.

The ray of wisdom when it shows itself in Air takes the form of the Air of pure mind. Air is in motion in all the places between heaven and earth. Air sees and knows from the vantage point of countless organs of perception. Air is more than the atmosphere; it is the solar wind, the sound of the turning of our galaxy, and the sound of the first moment. Pure mind contains all and is hindered by nothing.

The powers of Air, when called through the sponsorship of the three rays, generate much of what is the Craft of the Wise. These include invocation, evocation, true names, clear seeing, and all forms of mental magick. Communication with spirits and travel to other planes and realms is in Air's work. Divination and psychism are fostered by the ever-present and ever-perceptive Element of Air.

Libra, Aquarius, Gemini

The three Air signs describe how selfhood and personality are shaped by Air. Libra is cardinal air, so it is the Fire of Air. The Libra energy wants to rearrange things until they are in balance, in harmony, until they are aesthetically pleasing. It is the Air that seeks connections to others, wants to understand them, their lives, and their network of relationships. This energy seeks fairness and consistency of purpose.

Aquarius is fixed air, so it is the Air of Air. All Air signs use conceptualization and abstraction to make sense of the world, but for Aquarius, this is the primary mode of thought. Aquarius has the capacity to see the invisible guidelines and structures that shape society. This is the sign that sees with exactness and lucidity what would be ideal. Aquarius wants to make a world that matches its vision.

Gemini is mutable air, so it is the Water of Air. It flows through the world seeking to touch and taste everything. It is the Air that wishes to engage with every possibility. It is the restless wind that only knows itself while in motion. Gemini is the capacity to have dual consciousness of self and other self.

Yetzirah

This is the level where all thoughts, emotions, passions, and images take on detailed shapes and forms. Some of these thought-forms are durable, lasting for millennia, while others last only as long as a soap bubble.

Yetzirah is the world of formation, where that which will be made physical is acquiring the density and definition to be constructed. It is also the world in which all that was, might be, or almost was is in the boneyard, the warehouse, the library of ideas waiting to be recombined. Yetzirah is the eternal sky of clouds, changing shape and color, stirred or stilled by the powers of Air. Sometimes this is the astral plane, or the dreaming, or parts of the sideways realms such as those of the Fae. It is the place where the weather is also made of time and thought.

Air is the part of your soul and spirit that gives you the capacity to navigate in Yetzirah. Air is what gives you the ability to perceive what is in this world and to shape it. This is where the Air of inspiration enters you. Water makes it possible for Fire to be more manifest, and it is through Fire that the impetus of the Source is seen. The Air of Yetzirah takes all of the above and combines and delineates and balances them in the great thought, the great song of creativity.

Sacred Air

Breath and breathwork are essential to working with the powers of Air. There are many good resources and different approaches to working with breath. I encourage you to do some exploring, find what suits you, and do it until it becomes second nature. If you already include conscious breathing as a part of your practice, experiment with how you can add concepts about the Element of Air to that work.

Regardless of what your starting point may be, you can begin immediately by breathing with intention. If you need to analyze something, breathe in the Air of Aquarius with each breath. Or per-haps you need the Air of the ray of power so that you may speak with steadfast strength. The possibilities are as many as the attributes of Air.

When you are chanting, invoking, speaking sacred names, et cet-era, hear and feel the vibrations of your voice upon the Air. Then remind yourself that Air, and your subtle voice, exist on many planes and in many worlds. Reach out with your imagination, your mind, and speak those words again in the subtle places, and listen for your voice. Repeat this until you have reached as many levels as you can. Having become aware of the range of your many voices, say or chant again with all your voices as a chorus. Let Air carry your voice, send it forth that it might be heard by whomever must hear it. This is the magickal voice.

14

Earth

Earthing

Earth is both womb and tomb and the recycler of everything. Earth and the Earth plane are the natural destination for all the impulses from above. Earth and the Earth plane are the field of action for the exploration of the possible. Earth is form, information, and boundaries. The special boundaries of beginning, middle, and end belong to this Element. Earth is also where the foundation is laid for those impulses to recombine in new ways to ascend and enrich the above. Each of the Elements can be used for cleansing and healing, and Earth's style relies upon these qualities to bring about wholeness.

When you participate in grounding and centering practices, you are trusting that Earth will take whatever is in excess and deal with it in a good fashion. This is a recognition that the Earth is larger than you are and can easily absorb any excess energy. If you are lacking energy, it can grant it as well. Earth is more than a lightning or grounding rod. You are a microcosm relative to the macrocosm of the Earth. The greater momentum and memory of what balance should be is held within that larger macrocosm, and it reminds you of your proper state of being. The Element of Earth reminds you when to be a microcosm, a rhizome, or a holon. Simply standing barefoot or touching the ground with awareness and intention triggers the act of earthing.

There are many protocols in different systems that bury or pour things out to give them to Earth when their work is done, or they are no longer wholesome. Earth has the power to absorb unwanted energy and the ability to compost it as well. Earth has the power to take negative decay and turn it into the raw materials for positive renewal. Given enough time, Earth makes everything new again. Even the continents are pulled deep into the Earth to melt and be reborn in new times and shapes.

Embodiment

One of the most remarkable powers of Earth is, in a sense, a spiritualized form of gravity. The Element of Earth is what anchors essence into form. In beings such as ourselves, it is the power of Earth that holds and folds Ether, Spirit, and Quintessence into the layers of the subtle bodies, with the physical body as its center and lowest point. Earth is what makes incarnation possible.

Embodiment is not just limited to the physical plane. The forms, or vessels, of the spirits are organized and anchored by the Element of Earth in their plane of residence. The Element of Earth in its densest form in the lower planes has an organizing influence that extends upward through all the planes of the universe. It is Earth that is manifesting the manifest universe. Embodiment is also the way that beauty and the capacity to experience beauty comes into existence.

Fertility

As Spirit proceeds from the planes of being, it divides and apportions itself to become many from one source. This process is an unfolding and an elaboration that makes the implicit become explicit. It is a process of creation that fulfills what is but does not create something new.

Earth is always joining things together and compressing them into new combinations and forms. Earth is true fertility that creates ceaselessly without ever repeating itself. All things are unique combinations within specific locations and timeframes. Every rose is different from every other rose. Each crystal of quartz is quartz, but each is one of a kind and cannot be repeated. No song is sung the same twice. Life, whether it is biological, physical, or subtle, is ever changing.

The fertility of Earth ultimately arises with the tide of immanence and enriches the above. The descending tide of transcendence provides the abundance of materials that are the medium of Earth's fertility. There is a strange and wonderful reciprocity here in this universal ecology that spans many layers of reality. Fertility expresses itself in all things manifest, including but not limited to biology.

Evolution

When the never-ending fertility of Earth is placed within the constraints of time and the limits of form, adaptation and evolution become inevitable. The Element of Earth and the lower planes create the necessary conditions to explore, test, and learn. This applies to physical characteristics, personalities, cultures, and so on.

It is only through the challenges imposed by linear time, the wear and tear of physicality, and the limits of the senses of perception and awareness that evolution can function fully. What is learned and refined in the denser planes is what rises to enrich the upper planes. Spiritually, evolution is more than chance, trial, and selection, because the Element of Earth also holds the memory of what has been and might be. This becomes the guidance and foresight of the group mind of populations and species. Evolution follows the strictures and rules of matter but is steered, when possible, by spiritual patterns and forces.

Intuition and Instinct

The memory of the Element of Earth is embedded into the shapes, substances, arrangement, and timelines of all things in existence. Everything that is manifest is the culmination of countless interactions, materials, and moments that led to existence.

The Element of Earth within you bears the imprint and memory of manifest reality. This is the Element of form, pattern, and ordered information. Your genetic code, your epigenetics, the memories that lie outside your reach, and your perception of subtle energies are all within the compass of Earth.

Some of what is called intuition or instinct is the Element of Earth communicating the patterns and probabilities that are self-evident when perceived in the consciousness of Earth. Given the bustle and noise of normal waking consciousness it is no wonder that intuition and instinct often go unheard or overlooked. Practices that make space and silence within yourself will help to bring these gifts of guidance from the background to the foreground.

Three Earths

The ray of power when it shows itself in Earth takes the form of law manifest. These are not laws written as words or formulas, they are expressed by the shape of the world. These laws are in the pull of gravity and the spark of electricity. These are in the order apparent in a crystal, taking the shape that is encoded in its molecules, and in the synthesis of proteins in cells. Earth is both the lawgiver and the recipient of the law.

The ray of love when it shows itself in Earth takes the form of eternal return. With the patience of the Earth itself, nothing is ever lost or goes to waste. Everything is eventually returned to the cycles of birth, death, and rebirth. There are cycles within cycles that range from the smallest of things to the largest, with beginnings and endings that are but the left and the right hands of Earth. Seemingly the most rigid of the Elements, it is also the sponsor of the churn and the flux that is eternity expressed in matter.

The ray of wisdom when it shows itself in Earth takes the form of myriad forms. In part, this is the outrageous creativity of nature creating novel forms of life and landscapes, but it is more. It is the magick of the innumerable compositions of music that can be created from the finite keys of a piano. It is a dozen engineers coming up with three dozen solutions to provide a needed function. It is the seed and impetus of all hope that searches the realm of the ideal to find what is possible, and that is also the power of this Earth.

Capricorn, Taurus, Virgo

The three Earth signs describe how selfhood and personality are shaped by Earth. Capricorn is cardinal earth, so it is the Fire of Earth. Capricorn is the energy that descends the deepest, following the urges of its Element of Earth but goaded by Fire. It also remembers the brightness above so keenly that it longs to climb the path of return to the Source. This the passion of Capricorn to accomplish things in the realm of matter.

Taurus is fixed earth, so it is the Air of Earth. Taurus seems to move slowly, but this is a matter of judgment. The consciousness of Taurus is sensate and sensual and in communion with the richness of the Earth, so it moves at its own rate. This is the power to truly experience what is being offered in the lower planes. It is also the power to appreciate and discern the magickal nature of matter.

Virgo is mutable earth, so it is the Water of Earth. It is aware of every shift in the environment, both subtle and dense. Virgo seeks to find what is sustainable and enduring amidst the constant change of the world. The consciousness of Virgo is what polishes the jewel, selects the best seeds to plant, keeps the chronicle so that Earth might strive for perfection.

Assiah

This is the last in the four worlds model of the Qabala. This is the world of expression of action and the home of dense matter. It is the completion of the process of creation and the beginning of the process of evolution. It is the peak of individuation, not just of beings but also of the manifest universe itself. No two stars will ever be the same.

This is where time takes the form of individual moments without repetition. This is where the Element of Earth gives harbor and home to all the Elements and essences. Though physical, Assiah is more than we can perceive. This is more than a comment on the limits of human senses or our instruments of science; it is a reminder of a vastness that exceeds all comprehension. We can tell ourselves stories, in the styles of myth or science, that help extend our grasp, but they are at best summaries and at worst comforting distortions. The Earth of Assiah is the realm of limits, forms, and boundaries. One of the greatest limits is the limits of knowledge.

The Earth of you contains the pattern of reality and is linked to all the rest of Assiah without separation. The map is within you. The rules of the game are within you. The process of change and the creation of stability rest in Assiah. The matter of a plane is the thought of the plane above it. Conversely, the thought of one plane becomes the matter of the plane below it. Wherever this transition and exchange is present, both Assiah and the Element of Earth are in action. Remember not to be literal; Assiah and Earth are present on more than the plane of dense matter. Earth and Assiah can show you how to enter and exit form.

Sacred Earth

When you use salt, herbs, oils, crystals, candles, and the materials of magick, you are working with the Element of Earth in addition to any other reasons for which you may be employing those materials. The dense matter of the materials is the steward that holds their virtues. Simply adding an awareness, acknowledgment, and request for Earth to cooperate in your endeavors will yield better results. Placing your request for cooperation with the Earth of those materials will do even more. By extension, all the magickal tools and objects are also made of Earth, and respecting this part of them will expand their utility.

There are many forms of magick that are not body centric. Regardless of how large or little the role your physical body may play in your style of magick, recognizing the Earth of your body is important. The fuller your awareness of your physicality, the more power you will be able to raise and to shape without harm. With greater awareness of your power of Earth, you also gain the stability and the anchoring need to push, pull, and shape power without being blown away. Your capacity to send things forth or rise on the planes will be made easier by your full possession of your body, not less.

With this expanded and deepened connection to the physical world, it also becomes easier to perceive the sacred landscape that surrounds you. The world is buzzing with life and enchantment, but to access it, you must consciously become a part of it. It is the physical world that feeds the spirits; that should be enough of a clue to give more honor and credence to its power.

15

The Fifth Elements

Definitions

This chapter is called the Fifth Elements, because there is not just one version of the unity of the Elements, there are many. Of these many, there are three forms that are the keys to understanding them. I am defining my terms for these to share my insights, and these definitions may diverge from how you use these words.

Often, I have seen the words Ether, Spirit, and Quintessence used as if they were synonyms, but I view them as having three separate meanings and functions. For the sake of clarity, keep this in mind as you read the chapter. If you want to use your terms or create new ones, please do so but keep the distinctions in mind. Like the Four Elements, the Fifth Elements undergo phase changes as they pass through or exist in the various planes of being. Just as water can be a liquid, a gas, a solid, or a plasma, the Fifth Elements have comparable states as well.

Ether

The simplest definition for Ether is that it is the product of the unification of the Four Elements. As such, it is something that occurs in the denser planes of existence, so it is connected to the current of immanence and the rising current of return to the Source of all things.

Immanence is interpreted and described in a wide assortment of ways in different traditions and religions, but the largest area of agreement is that spirit and/or the divine are present in all that exists in the manifest universe. For some, this means that God/gods/goddesses and such arise from the material world. For others, it means that the divine and the other planes of existence are fully integrated with the physical realm. There are many other interpretations as well, but for the purpose of the Elements, it is the tide of immanence that allows that which has been separated to rejoin.

When speaking of Ether, just like the Elements, it can express as a local, global, or universal phenomena. Ether functions within the framework of time and the laws of the manifest universe. It is important to point out that this framework is more than linear time and more than just physical laws; it includes metaphysical extensions to these. Ether is everlasting, sempiternal, but is not outside some form of time. This is one of the reasons I associate Ether with the soul; that is to say, the unique being that exists as an incarnation. One of the other phases that Ether can take is called prana, chi, or life force.

If we zoom in on the process of the Elements uniting to become Ether, the procedure is more accurately seen as the union of the sixteen sub-Elements becoming four, then the four becoming one. For example, in the Element of Water, the Air of Water, the Fire of Water, the Water of Water, and the Earth of Water join to form the Ether of Water. The same process occurs in the other Elements. It is the sub-Ethers of the Four Elements that unite to form Ether.

It is common for this to be referred to as the Spirit of Water, and so on, but I think this is hides access to understanding the full process. It would be more precise to call this the Ether of Water, Ether of Fire, et cetera, but that is not a common practice. Ethers of Elements are the equivalents of the lower self or enlivening soul of those beings that are elementals. The Ethers of the Elements are what sponsor the unification of smaller portions of elemental consciousness to construct hive minds and many of the beings that we identify as elementals.

Spirit

The simplest definition for Spirit is that it is the source material for the Four Elements. Spirit is like white light that, as it passes through the prism of the planes, reveals the colors that are the Four Elements. Spirit is connected to transcendence and the downward current of manifestation and differentiation.

The transcendent aspect of Spirit or of God/gods/goddesses is sometimes presented as existing outside time and space and unbounded by the laws of nature. Transcendence and immanence are sometimes presented as mutually exclusive as well, though that is not my conclusion. In the context of the Elements, it is more useful to conceptualize them as the top and bottom of a continuum. Moreover, the downward and upward tendencies of Spirit and Ether result in a turning wheel of cycles.

With regard to the idea that Spirit's transcendence places it outside the boundaries of knowledge or laws, there is another way to explain its properties that is more useful for practitioners of magick. As Spirit descends, it divides and expands to become all things, including laws both physical and metaphysical. As such, Spirit is not separate from the parameters of time and space, because those parameters are made of, derived from, Spirit itself.

However, within the strictures of denser planes, only some of those parameters may exist at once, and what cannot be made coherent is canceled. Spirit contains more possible laws and properties than can be manifested in any given framework of the denser planes. The nature of manifest reality, including laws both metaphysical and physical, is another way in which Spirit incarnates/substantiates itself. When it appears that Spirit has acted outside the laws of time and space, it is more productive to view this as an instance where other parameters have been swapped in.

It is the downward, toward denser planes, motion of Spirit—with its consequent division into the Elements—that is the primary driver

of manifestation in the physical world. In the process of differentiat-
ing itself, Spirit divides into the Spirit of each Element. To my way of
thinking, these may properly be called the Spirit of Water, Spirit of
Fire, and so on. These are the equivalents of the higher self or divine
spark components of those beings that are elementals. These are the
crucial parts of those beings we identify as higher order elementals,
such as, but not limited to, the monarchs and other individuated
elementals.

Quintessence

The word "quintessence" has a variety of meanings in herbalism, physics, and other fields, in addition to its use as a word to denote a perfect
example or another word for Ether. I am adding additional meanings
to this word, as I have not found one in usage that meets the needs for
this purpose. In this case, Quintessence is the third form of the Fifth
Element that comes into being when rising Ether meets descending
Spirit. It is nether immanent nor transcendent, though it may have
qualities of both or neither.

Quintessence is like the boundary between water and oil in a glass
vessel; the effects of the boundary are clearly visible, but the substance
of the boundary is not. Quintessence is present wherever there is a
meeting of Ether and Spirit; this is at every boundary of the veils,
and auric sheaths, and planar boundaries. There are myriad meetings
of the upward and downward tides of Ether and Spirit that generate
Quintessence. They present themselves at all available microcosmic,
mesocosmic, and macrocosmic levels of scale.

The Four Elements are the building blocks for manifest reality;
whereas Quintessence is the material that provides the partitions and
connections to articulate manifest reality. Quintessence is also strongly
associated with the middle self and is a key point of overlap in the
nature of humans and that of elementals. It is what bridges mind and
brain, as well as beingness and consciousness.

Often, the work of psychism, spellwork, and ritual are in the domain of Quintessence. Just like the Four Elements, this is always in action when you do any form of divination, magick, psychic work, and so on. When you are aware of the joining and the interaction of Ether and Spirit within yourself, you awaken the capacity to work with the power of Quintessence with greater ease and control.

From a metaphysical perspective, it can be said that everything that is manifest is imbued with a degree of life and with one or more versions of the Fifth Element. Whether your view is closer to animism, pantheism, panentheism, or something else that includes the assertion that all manifest things have life and the Fifth Element, there is the distinction that is made between organic and inorganic in current science that needs to be addressed.

Another point to consider is that life and death are not a binary from a magickal perspective. Varying proportions of the quantities and the arrangements of Ether, Spirit, and Quintessence create the spectrum of possibilities that can encompass these ranges. Consciousness and self-awareness can be organized and function in many ways throughout these ranges of possibilities. The expression of consciousness and self-awareness is also modified by what their bodies or vessels are made of and whether it is dense or subtle.

It is Quintessence that is the Element most responsible for what humans consider to be consciousness and self-awareness. Waking consciousness is the rippling surface between the upwelling depths of the soul and the descending eternal Spirit within each person. Thought and communication with elementals, or other spiritual entities, is powered by Ether, understood by Spirit, and mediated by Quintessence.

Properties That Apply to the Three

The Four Elements each have numerous attributes, tendencies, preferred states of existence, influences and functions on material things, and so on. It is by these attributes that they can be quickly identified.

On the other hand, the Fifth Elements are formless yet remain coherent and self-organizing because their properties are self-emergent. The Fifth Elements are also dimensionless, and because of this, they can expand or contract without gaining or losing capacity or integrity. The Fifth Elements have no actual polarity, so they also have the power to attract, to repel, and to remain neutral.

When I was first taught about the Elements in a magickal context, one of the basic attributes for Spirit (which was the term applied to all three) was that it was both the circumference and the center of things. This seems a logical outgrowth of being dimensionless. To many, the word "dimensionless" implies something that is infinitesimally small. It is better to compare the concept to both the timelessness of eternity and to the sempiternal state which is of infinite duration. Every place contains the Fifth Elements and is functionally the center point of its universe. All physical reality is surrounded by the Fifth Elements, and they form the boundaries, so they are the circumference as well.

Ether, Spirit, and Quintessence can also appear as particles, waves, and fields. They can express themselves as gradations of presence, from barely noticeable to overwhelming the senses. They can be binary and discrete, or they can have blurry boundaries and multiple phases. They can change from fully anchored to dense physical matter to being completely unfettered.

The Fifth Elements have all the degrees of motion and change and more than that which exists for the Four Elements. This may seem self-evident but is often forgotten. The Fifth Element (or Elements) is both singular and plural as needed by the circumstances and/or the planes in which it is in action. The mystery of the three in one of most trinities applies here.

Tools

The tools that I use to represent the Fifth Elements in the sacred regalia are the cauldron and the egg. Both tools inherently have the properties of holding and containing. Both have transformative qualities as well. The cauldron brings to mind processes such as steeping, cooking, melting, smelting, and such. The egg suggests the generative power of a spark of life, both organizing and shaping matter to bring about life and as a vessel for that life.

These properties are in line with the ideas related to Ether, Spirit, and Quintessence. These tools can be used separately, but I have gotten good results when placing an egg inside a cauldron for working or rituals. I have use crystal eggs, wooden eggs, and living eggs, depending upon the work at hand.

Some Useful Glyphs for the Fifth Elements

It is useful to have glyphs and symbols to represent the Four Elements for magick, visualization, scribing, and notation. There is a glyph for Spirit that is frequently used that is a circle with internal spokes like a wheel. The number of spokes varies, with eight being the most prevalent. This glyph is useful because it has been used by many people and has a well-established thoughtform, but it lacks specificity.

Spirit
(Standard Symbol)

I have created my own glyphs to reflect a threefold understanding of the Fifth Elements. At this point, the unique nature of the three versions should be clear, and the need for separate glyphs made apparent. In chapter 4, I included a figure that summarizes the interplay of the Four Elements and the Fifth Elements.

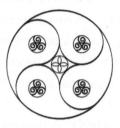

From this figure, I derived the glyph for Spirit, which is a four-pointed star made of arcs, and the glyph for Ether, which is a circle with four lobes. The glyph for Quintessence is the glyph of Ether within Spirit.

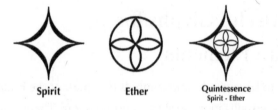

Spirit   **Ether**   **Quintessence**
Spirit - Ether

These glyphs can be used as focal points for concentrating your mind on perceiving the Fifth Elements within yourself. They can be scribed as energy in ritual work or onto candles or paper to facilitate communication with elemental beings. They can be envisioned and energized over oils, incenses, et cetera to firmly anchor Ether, Spirit, or Quintessence within them. I have also used them as components in sigils, amulets, and other magickal workings.

The Fifth Elementals

The elementals that are ordinarily called upon are the sylphs of the Air, the salamanders of Fire, the undines of Water, and the gnomes of Earth.

That there are no Elements without elementals seems like an obvious statement, but it is one that has not been fully realized until recently.

In the last decade or so, I and some of my colleagues have been having encounters with a hitherto undescribed type of elemental. These elementals appear to be composed of the Fifth Elements, with a preponderance of Quintessence in the ones with which we've had successful communication. They appear to vary widely in size, degree of individuation, and all the other variables that are present in the more familiar elementals.

These Fifth Elementals are enlivened by Ether in the form of prana/life force, but their forms are made of what comes into being when the rising Element of Ether (immanent tide) meets the descending Element of Spirit (transcendent tide). It is this interaction at every boundary of the veils, and auric sheaths, and planar boundaries that is what their equivalent of a body is made from.

It is my belief that these elementals have always been present. Perhaps they are being encountered now because something is changing in humans, or it is an artifact of the changing of the Age, or the elementals have their own reasons for initiating contact. The elementals have their own wills, agendas, and hopes. There are many other things that could be speculated upon, but more accounts of interactions need to be gathered before reasonable conclusions can be drawn. I encourage you to make your own attempts to become aware of the elementals of the Fifth Elements.

I can share my preliminary findings and observations on these beings. There is a strong association between these elementals and ley lines, vortices, and other places where the life of the Earth is flowing strongly or is concentrated. They can take many shapes, but I often perceived them as sinuous forms that resemble snakes, braided flows of liquid, draconic outlines, and geometric patterns.

The sinuous forms have caused some of my colleagues to use names such as "naga" or "wyrm" as provisional terminology until a

consensus develops around what to call them. The problem with calling them nagas or wyrms, and similar names, in addition to being
confusing, is that those beings' nature and lore does not apply. For the
moment, I generally refer to them as the fifth elementals or the pranic
elementals.

Because these elementals are made of the Fifth Elements, they
could be called upon to do things that the elementals of Air, Fire,
Water, and Earth cannot do as easily or fully. Since prana, life force,
is one of their primary constituents, there are a wide range of healing
applications to be explored.

Since Quintessence is the material that gives them form and presence, it is very likely that these elementals might have greater ease in
opening and closing the portals between the planes. The inclusion of
the fifth elementals in creating sacred space, containers for workings,
is a logical extension to current practices.

I have been experimenting with working with these elementals as
aides in communicating with spirits that are not of the Elements and
have had good results. I have also been experimenting with awakening the fifth elementals that dwell within me for work with my three
selves, as well as my personal Four Elements. If you choose to experiment with these, please take notes and read them regularly.

The Element of Time

It is my belief that the Fifth Elements are also the Elements of the
collection of phenomena that are jointly referred to as time. The Fifth
Elements are associated with the various planes of being, as well as
interpenetrating all of space, so they must also be associated with time.

There is not one kind of time but many. Time can be described
as flowing like a river. Time can be described like an ocean, with all
of time being present at once. Time can be experienced as moving at
different rates and in different frames of reference. Time can be seen

as a field of possibilities. Time can be seen as unchangeable. The Fifth Elements are capable of bridging and harmonizing all the possible forms of time.

It has been widely reported that time is experienced as moving at different rates or functioning differently in the various planes of existence. There is also a well-accepted premise that as you rise on the planes, things become more rarified; as you descend, they become denser.

All five of the Elements also follow this pattern of being denser or more subtle in accordance with the plane they occupy. The Fifth Elements have the lowest and the highest reach within the planes of manifest reality. The many behaviors of time can be explained as variations in the density of the Fifth Elements at different planes of existence.

Let's do a thought experiment to better conceptualize this possibility. Imagine that time is a fluid that is being pushed by the upward tide of Ether and the downward tide of Spirit. Imagine that at the level of physical reality, time is like a river of honey. Even if you were a strong swimmer, you would be carried along by the thick current from the past to the future.

Imagine rising on the planes; now the river of time is only as thick as water. Depending on your strength and that of the current, you could make headway against the current going backward or perhaps go forward faster than the flow.

If you rise again, perhaps the river is as thin as mist, and you can move with ease in any direction. In this subtle form of time, you can feel the currents but are not controlled by them. You can move not only backward and forward but also right and left to explore probabilities.

Rise again and you may find that you've reached the end of the river and are floating in a shimmering sea of light in the all at once. Whether you do divination, past-life work, time magick, or comparable things, consider what options are available when you work with the Elements of time.

We will return to more on the Fifth Elements later in the book, as they relate to particular theories, constructs, and teachings. It would be productive to take some time now before proceeding to refresh your memory on the previous chapters. It is especially valuable to review chapter 8 on the threefold way. As an exercise, work again with the column of light that connects the three selves. This time, try to experience how Ether, Spirit, and Quintessence function throughout the column of light.

16

An Elemental Healing Ritual

This is a relatively short ritual that can be done by a solo practitioner or a group of up to forty people or so. It can be done as a stand-alone rite or as the conclusion to a sequence of elemental workings or meditations. It can be used to support and to hasten physical healing, but it works well for emotional release and healing as well. Perhaps its most important use is as a ritual to encourage the alignment of the three selves to the Elements.

Regardless of what intentions are applied to this ritual, it helps to strengthen the central column of energy in the participants and the interactions between Ether, Spirit, and Quintessence. As in the previous ritual, the annotations with instructions for the person conducting the ritual are in italics.

The Four Becoming One

I. Purification

We purify at the entry to the ritual with saltwater and incense, and we gaze into a scrying mirror to see ourselves as whole and how we aspire to be. Enter and move to form a circle or concentric circles, as needed.

If it is small group, you can use an altar with saltwater, incense, and a mirror so that people can manage it on their own. If it is a larger group, having attendants assist with these items as people enter will make the process smoother. The saltwater, incense, and mirror should be blessed and prepared before people gather for the ritual.

II. Cast and Call

Beginning in the east, the elemental gates are opened with calls to the elemental monarchs that dwell in the Elements. The scribing of the circle boundary is done as a part of circling to perform the calls. All respond with,

> *"Hail and Welcome."*
> *We are declared between the worlds, and all say,*
> *"Blessed Be."*

If it is not your practice, or you do not wish to use a circle casting, you may modify this part of the ritual. In adjusting the setting of a container for the work, you must include requests for the elemental monarchs to be present. These calls may be brief or lengthy as befits your needs and style, but they must include statements on how the monarchs are to assist the work of the ritual. It is important to create a boundary, because it will help to focus the energy of the ritual.

III. Honoring the Elements

We turn to each of the compass directions, and we honor its Element with a chant. Each chant is repeated until it feels right. Suggestions for the chants are at the end of the chapter.

I am a great believer in the power of chanting in ritual to raise energy and to alter consciousness. Feel free to use your own chants if you so desire. Another option is to offer poetry or dance for each Element. The critical part of this step in the ritual is offering gifts of energy to the Elements. It is also vital that each person in the ritual participate in some fashion.

IV. Awakening the Elements within the Selves

Each of the Elements is activated in the lower self, the middle self, and the higher self. This is done in the central column of energy (middle pillar). Focus your awareness at the base of your spine, the root. Use your voice to slowly drone the Elements,

"Air, Fire, Water, Earth."

As you do so, visualize a symbol associated with each Element. Repeat this process with your focus on your heart, then with the focus on the crown of your head. In the transition between doing the work in lower, middle, and higher parts of the column, take a few slow breaths.

You may use the triangle-based symbols, the tattva symbols, the tools of the sacred regalia, or physical depictions, such as a drop, a stone, et cetera. What is important is that you combine the name, a visual cue, and a location for the selves on the central column. Take your time with this step, as it is the foundation of this working.

V. Calling the Spirits of Elements Within

We face the east, stretch out our arms, and draw the Spirit of Air into ourselves. Hug yourself to bring it in. We face the south, stretch out our arms, and draw the Spirit of Fire into ourselves. Hug yourself to bring it in or bring your hands in to your chest. We face the west, stretch out our arms, and draw the Spirit of Water into ourselves. Hug yourself to bring it in. We face the north, stretch out our arms, and draw the Spirit of Earth into ourselves. Hug yourself to bring it in.

This step can be done in silence or with minimal verbal instruction should you deem it necessary. If it is a larger group that needs a bit of coordinating, you may wish to have people intone, "Spirit of Air Come!" several times followed by "Blessed Be!" and so on for each Element. Depending upon your situation, you may wish to have altars or banners for each of the Elements to help focus attention and energy.

VI. Request for Healing and Integration

Next, face the center of the ritual space. Envision a pillar of light that reaches deep into the ground and far up into the sky. See the pillar filling with so much light as to be opaque with brilliance. Then turn your attention inwards and become aware of the central column of energy within you. Pay attention to the flow of light up and down your personal pillar of light. Feel the resonance between the two pillars of light. Then, silently or aloud, make whatever request for healing, growth, or integration that you may need. Pause and wait for a feeling of acknowledgment.

Depending upon who is present in the ritual, there may be a need to offer more guidance and explanation about the central column of energy. It is also valuable to encourage people to offer brief and focused requests rather than lengthy lists or options. There will be other opportunities to do further work; it is better to do one smaller thing fully. If you like, you may also wish to have a central altar with emblems of the Elements and a central candle in glass.

VII. The Four Becoming One

The group circles slowly clockwise and all chant:

> Air I Am, Fire I Am,
> Water, Earth, And Spirit I Am[2]

As you chant, focus energy toward the pillar of light in the center. When the energy peaks, stop circling and transition to freeform toning and release the energy into the central pillar. Envision a shower or radiation of energy from the center onto and into you. Allow some time for the energy to settle in before proceeding.

If there are people in the ritual with mobility concerns, encourage them to imagine that they are circling around the center as they chant. Note that there is no instruction to hold hands during the circling. Indeed, it is better not to hold hands, as there is greater benefit if the

---

2   Andras Corban Arthen, EarthSpirit Community © 1982, *www. youtube.com*

energy exchange is between just the individuals and the central pillar. You may substitute a different chant or use only toning, but you must raise energy by using your voice and/or breath.

VIII. Thanks and Closing

The pillar of light in the center of the ritual is dismissed. It becomes blurry and dissolves away. Words of thanks are offered to each of the Four Elements and the monarchs individually. All say, "We Give Thanks!" for each of these. Then offer words of thanks and gratitude for the healings and blessings received. The circle or ritual container is released and dismissed according to how it was created. The ritual ends with words such as,

> *"The Circle Is Open but Unbroken.*
> *Merry Meet and Merry Part*
> *And Merry Meet Again."*

Make sure that everyone is fully grounded, centered, and back to a balanced state of being. The release and dismissal of the ritual container should match the pattern used at the beginning of the ritual. It is essential that you release the central pillar before dismissing the container.

Element Honoring Chants

If you would like to listen to these chants for free, they are all available online on my website as well as on the Assembly of the Sacred Wheel's site. They can also be purchased as downloads or on CDs. Of course, these are just suggestions, and there are many other chants or poems for the Elements that you could use in this ritual.

East (Air)

"Sylph Song"

Airy Messenger Clear the Clouds
From Our Minds
Whispers in the Winds
Words Rustle Through the Leaves
Inspiration Spins Like Feathers in the Winds
Sweet Air, We Breath Deep
New Promises We Keep

—Ivo Dominguez, Jr.

South (Fire)

"Fire Soul"

Fire, Fire Soul's Desire
Changer Change Me
Burning, Burning, Higher

—Ivo Domínguez, Jr., with Paula Fasbenner for the "Gathering of
Salamanders" Ritual at Autumn Magick 1993

West (Water)

"Waters of Life"

Water
Waters of Life
Gentle Rain, Soft Mist,
And Tidal Pools.
Hot Beating Blood
Cool Ocean Deeps
Water of Wonder

Mystery of Our Hearts
Water of Wonder
Mystery of Our Hearts
—Ivo Dominguez, Jr.

North (Earth)

"Earth Spirits Chant"

Guardians of the Dreamtime,
Shapes and Forms.
Roots of the Mountain,
Silent and Deep.
Earth Spirits Dreaming,
Awaken to Our Touch.
Shapers of the Crystal,
Shapers of the Leaf,
Shapers of the Valley
Beneath Our Feet.

—Jim E. Dickinson, Ivo Domínguez, Jr., Michael G. Smith,
Nancy G. Stewart, and James C. Welch
(written during the ice storm of 1994 at Seelie Court)

17

The Elements:
Depths and Heights

The Elements have different attributes, behaviors, and appearances at different planes of reality. Usually, the focus in examining them is on how to perceive or to make use of the Elements in their various phases and forms. The idea that the Elements are the building blocks of the universe is widespread, and though a useful idea, this leads to the neglect of another idea.

The Elements are more than building blocks, they are the architecture of the universe. They are the foundations, buttresses, domes, and spires of reality. The Elements are configured in structures that reach from the depths to the heights of the planes of being. When you pull back and look at them through a wider perspective, the blocks blur, and the architectural Elements become apparent.

"The Sun Beyond the Sun"

The Sun Beyond the Sun
The Sun Within the Earth
Bright Sun, Dark Sun We Are One
I Am a Breath of the Sun
I Am a Spark of the Sun
I Am a Tear of the Sun
I Am Golden, I Am Gold

—Ivo Dominguez, Jr.,
on the "Awakening the Dream" chant CD

This is a chant that I've used for many purposes, one of which is to connect with larger Elemental structures. If you'd like to listen to this, you can do so through my website or other online sources. In this chant, the sun beyond the sun is a reference to the organizing and enlivening principle that is the beginning and ongoing source of the manifest universe. It is not the bright ball of fusion fire at the center of our solar system.

The sun within the earth is a reference to how the energy and essence of creation dwell within dense matter. The last lines declare alignment and identification with the organizing and enlivening principle symbolized by the sun. If you are willing, repeat these lines out loud a few times before continuing this chapter. If you have the time and inclination, listen to it online so that you can chant it. Consider using it as a warm-up before working with or contemplating the depths and the heights in your practices.

The Anchors of Being

I have often envisioned the Four Elements as colossal pillars that rise through the planes of reality. This is an image that shows up in many guises in different cultures and stories, such as in Egyptian, Greek, and Norse mythologies. The pillars are sometimes personified as guardians or upholders. They show up as the four heavenly kings in China, the watchtowers in Enochian magick, the royal stars of Persia, the four sons of Horus, the dwarves at the directions—Austri, Vestri, Nordri, and Sudri—and more.

Many of these stories and images speak of holding up the sky or offering benevolent protection or bringing balance. These myths and cosmologies also inspire the layout of sacred cities, temples, and ritual spaces. To me, this speaks of the role of the Elements in keeping reality from collapsing back into its unitary state. It is the Elements that push against the void to make space and time within each plane, in addition to holding each layer apart and stable.

I think that the Elements also moor and fasten spirit to matter, soul to body, mind to brain, supernal impulse to manifest action, and so on. The basic predispositions of Fire to ascend, Water to descend, Air to distribute, and Earth to compress make it possible for there to be a mixing of essences, energy, and matter of various densities that would otherwise separate and stratify. The mixing and fastening are held in a balance that is very much like that of living beings.

The process of life, whether organic or otherwise, is antientropic, maintains equilibriums that would fail without tending, and creates new order out of chaos. The entire manifest universe is alive, and its life is made possible by the Elements' ability to create order and balance within a changing field of possibilities and probabilities. Whether an essence is born into flesh or into the light-body of a divine being, the process of incarnation or the investiture into a god-form is mediated by the processes and powers of the Elements.

Four Great Beings

The four fixed-modality signs are Taurus, Leo, Scorpio, and Aquarius, whose Elements are Earth, Fire, Water, and Air, respectively. If you take into account their fixed modalities, they become the Airs of Earth, Fire, Water, and Air.

These are the signs whose midpoints anchor the holy days that are between the solstices and equinoxes: Beltane, Lammas, Samhain, and Imbolc. The cross-quarter days mark the peak of the seasonal energetic tides. They also mediate the power of the changes that come into being at the zero-degree points of the solstices and equinoxes. It is the neutrality of their Air sub-Element that makes this possible.

The bull is the emblem for Taurus. The lion is the emblem for Leo. The eagle is the key emblem for Scorpio. A human being is the emblem for Aquarius. If you combine the shapes of these four beings into one, you come up with the shape of the sphinx. The sphinx is a representation of the Elements joining to become Ether. The sphinx holds a special meaning as the completion of the great work that will be touched upon in the next chapter. These are also the four beings at the corners of the world card in many tarot decks.

These emblems are one of many iterations and echoes of the idea of four great beings engaged in maintaining the worlds. These beings are sometimes seen as separate and sometimes combined into tetramorphs with four faces or other combinations and arrangements. One example is the Mesopotamian *lammasu,* who are protective beings; this protective quality is a recurrent feature in these composite forms. These types of beings show up in the biblical prophet Ezekiel's vision of living creatures, as cherubim, and are later reimagined as the four Evangelists as well.

All these variations are connected with the protection, maintenance, and functioning of whatever plane, location, or spiritual niche in which they are stationed. Although the archangels have associations with Elements and directions, these are not their primary roles or functions. They are another order of being.

Although described somewhat differently in Judaism and Christianity, there is a shared story of four living creatures that surround the throne of their god. In Islam, the number of beings is not given, but they are in similar roles in the throne room of heaven. These are not my faiths, but a mystic vision is a mystic vision. I have had my own visions that are in line with the mythic truth of this story, if not the theology.

In the throne room vision, these beings are singing praise, holding the throne, and shielding the world from a blinding brilliance that would be too much. In my vision, these are not angels, archangels, or living creatures. They are the first emanations of when Spirit divided to form the Four Elements. They are more than the elemental monarchs, because contained within themselves is the totality of their Element. These four great beings remain at the boundary between time and eternity, anchoring, maintaining, and focusing the flow of both Spirit and the boundary to ensure the manifestation of the universe.

Because patterns repeat, like wheels within wheels, gears meshed with gears, and RNA to DNA, I believe that at each plane, level, and location—real, virtual, or imaginal—there are beings that are the descendants and avatars of the four great beings. In each setting, they do the work that is comparable and equivalent to that of the four great beings but modified to fit the localized needs. Collectively, these beings form and direct the great structures that are the architecture of existence. There is an echo of this present in any ritual, working, or construct that calls upon a set of four of any kind. Being aware of the role of these beings, whether explicitly referenced or not, can strengthen the castings, sacred space, or containers for magick that you create.

The Central Column

The concept of an axis that connects the above and the below is pervasive and highly variable. This is the world tree in all its alternative expressions. This is the path of life force that encircles and/or fills the line created by the spine. This is the middle pillar of the Qabala. It is the axis mundi and the omphalos, the umbilical cord of the world. It is also the Stupa of the purified elements in Buddhism. It is also the Asherah pole, the Irminsul, the Jupiter Column, the Djed Pillar, and so forth.

Please note, I am not suggesting that these are all the same thing, as each has its meaning and context within their cultures of origin and communities of practice. What I am proposing is that these are all interpretations of a spiritual truth that is larger than any one image can depict. They are each one dot, one pixel, in a vast panoramic vision.

In addition to the purposes and qualities offered by all these depictions of the central column, I ask you to also view the central column as the place where the Elements reunite to become Ether. This central column is also the conduit through which Spirit descends. In the central column, the meeting of the two streams not only creates Quintessence but also generates a spiraling current and a turning cycle. This brings to mind the caduceus and the Ida, Pingala, and Sushumna nadis of yoga.

From an elemental perspective, this central column also acts like an axle and hub. It is one of the structures made of the Elements that preserve order and function in the universe. It holds the center and gives it motion, which is essential to life. When you call upon or acknowledge this axis of the above and the below in your practices, remember that it also brings the power to hold things together. It is what balances the centrifugal and centripetal forces and brings stability. It is the flywheel and the gyroscope of reality. If you need a resilient casting, a strong container to hold and focus power during an intense working, the central column in an important ally.

The central column also contains the sequences of elemental beings. The crown or throne at the top of the column is pure Spirit. The top of the column is also the root and beginning of all the Elements. Time is not linear at that level of reality, so next to and simultaneous with the brilliance that is the source, crown, and throne are four great beings. Then lower on the column, there is the sphinx, which is the rising summation of the Elements that will become one and is the one in a different form.

Continuing down the central column, you find the elemental monarchs followed by elementals of all sizes and degrees of individuation, and so on. At bottom of the central column, there is also a throne and a crown, but its light cannot be seen, for it is fully invested in the world of matter.

We began this chapter with a chant, and it also comes to bear here. The sun beyond the sun is at the top of the central column and is indeed that brilliance. This light cannot exist until there is an elevation of awareness. The sun within the Earth is the at the bottom of the central column, and its light cannot be seen because its powers are turned inward to create physicality. This is the light as the compressive power of Earth.

You may have noticed in the chapter on the sub-Elements that when we look at the signs in astrology, there is no Earth of Earth, Earth of Fire, Earth of Water, or Earth of Air. Those sub-Elements rule the lowest portion of the central column and are the powers of the sun within the Earth. The sun and stars within the Earth are not the same as the ones in the heavens.

Travelers of the Depths and Heights

One of the gifts of being human is the capacity to move your awareness to different levels of the depths and heights. Having the fourfold nature and the threefold nature means that it is possible to communicate and work with a wide range of beings. The more you travel these realms that are real, virtual, and functional constructs of the imagination, the more you begin to build your own map and compass for further travel.

You also begin to take note of the travels and territories of other beings and to see that their shapes, the vessels that house their essence, vary in function and appearance from level to level. You also notice the beings that are the stalwarts, that stay put to do their work. All these things and more occur only if you make the choice to be aware and pay attention.

On many occasions, I have taken people walking in the woods where I live. Many but not all comment on the sense of peace and beauty—and the bugs, depending upon the season. If that is all they have to say, I begin to point out what they are missing as we walk. I point out the scrape on the tree from antlers, the lady slippers and trillium blooming low to the ground, the opossum in the tree, the hawk quietly circling high above, the box turtle near the path, and so on. Once pointed out, most begin to look more carefully and discover an entire landscape hidden under the autopilot expectations of what they would see. The same can be said of traveling the greater structures of the Elements.

Expectations can limit perception, even when those expectations are rooted in truths and general observations. There is a teaching that as you rise on the planes, there is a continuum of change from the highly detailed, concrete, and bounded norms of the lowest plane to the highly symbolic, rarefied, and boundless norms of the highest planes we can reach. In the lower planes, things still have analogues and references to the physical, so are more immediately intelligible. The higher you go, the more things become symbolic, until what is perceived is abstractions of color. This is mostly correct but can also prevent you from perceiving what is before you.

If you had been sitting in a darkened room to nap for a few hours, then stepped outside into the noonday sun, you'd probably squint or close your eyes. They would need to adapt to the brightness before you could see properly. If we reverse the scenario, and you step from a brightly lit room to the very dark outdoors, you would see little. Once again, given time your eyes would adapt, and you'd be able to pick out shapes and details.

When you venture into other planes and realms, allow your psychic senses to adapt to the local conditions. What appear as nothing but swooshes of brightness or color may resolve into details with some adaptation time. Also reexamine your expectations of what you will encounter and pay attention to what is present, not just what you've been told to expect.

Perception relies heavily on past experiences, expectations, and cues. Depending upon your background and experiences, you may or may not have a storehouse of data and previous impressions to rely upon in other states of reality. However, you are also made of the Elements, and they have access through their chain of being, through their connections, to offer you guidance. All the work that you do with the Elements and elementals can lead to having the frames of reference needed to better resolve the other realms. The more you work with Ether, Spirit, and Quintessence, the easier it will be to travel the depths and heights.

18

The Witches' Pyramid

In his book *Dogme et Rituel de la Haute Magie,* Éliphas Lévi wrote:

> *To attain the Sanctum Regnum (the sacred kingdom), in other words, the knowledge and power of the Magi, there are four indispensable conditions—an intelligence illuminated by study, an intrepidity which nothing can check, a will which cannot be broken, and a prudence which nothing can corrupt and nothing intoxicate. To know, to dare, to will, to keep silence—such are the four words of the Magus, inscribed upon the four symbolical forms of the Sphinx.*

The four words he specifies are often referred to as the powers of the magus or the powers of the sphinx. Aleister Crowley added a fifth power, the power to go, in *Liber Aleph* and expanded on his ideas on the powers in *Magick without Tears.* Writings by Éliphas Lévi (Alphonse Louis Constant) in 1854 and Crowley's expansion in the first part of the 20th century would eventually become the basis for the Witches' Pyramid sometime in the 1950s or 1960s.

I have not found a clear origin or originator for the Witches' Pyramid, but Leo Louis Martello, Paul Huson, and Lady Sheba's writings on the topic are the earliest I have seen. There is always the possibility that the earliest version was taught orally or held in unpublished or oathbound materials. Over the years, these "power" ideas passed through many traditions and evolved into a template and a paradigm for operative magick and personal development. I am aware of some witchcraft traditions that plot these powers onto a pentagram instead of a pyramid. This is fine for most of the purposes involving the powers of the magus/sphinx but excludes some of valuable options in ritual work.

In the Witches' Pyramid, Air is the power to know, Fire is the power to will, Water is the power to dare, Earth is the power to be silent. The power to go is associated with Spirit, but to my way of thinking it is the Fifth Elements. The placements for the powers and their associated Element at the points of the pyramid vary from tradition to tradition. In some, the placements match the directions used in their pattern for creating sacred space. In others, they match the positions related to the four fixed signs of the zodiac.

The system I use places Fire opposite Water, Air opposite Earth, thus pairing the primary and secondary Elements. The pyramid shape is also reminiscent of the cone of power, which is a vortex of power that is raised and sent forth in many witchcraft traditions.

The Witches' Pyramid is commonly taught as a template to make sure that a spell or ritual has all the parts needed for success. You must know what you are trying to accomplish and hold it clearly in the mind. This is the power of Air expressed as the power to know. You must have the will and the drive to guide the working to completion so that it comes into being. This is the power of Fire expressed as the power to will. You must keep silent so that you may listen for guidance and instinct and to avoid the calling of opposition to your work. This is the power of Earth expressed as the power to keep silent. You must have the strength of heart to believe you will succeed and to empower your work. This is the power of Water expressed as the power to dare. The release of a spell, sending it forth, is the power to go and become manifest. This is the power of the Fifth Elements expressed as the power to go.

The simplest method to use the Witches' Pyramid, beyond using it as a psychological checklist, is to call on each of the Elements to lend support to its assigned power. This is an action that is separate from calling the Elements to create sacred space. If your ritual or spell uses materials, make sure the ingredients or tools have been charged with the part they have to play. Then, both consciousness and energy are raised to form and send forth the cone of power.

I often envision the Witches' Pyramid beginning to spin around me until it is moving so quickly that it blurs into the cone. The concentration and release of the power at the tip are the acts of becoming dimensionless like the Fifth Elements. In that dimensionless state, the working may go wherever it must to fulfill its purpose.

The four powers of the magus or sphinx, with the addition of the fifth power, also can be applied for personal and spiritual development. Becoming aware of the Elements within yourself and bringing them into proper relationships and proportions is a well-established practice for personal development. The addition of the words from the powers of the Witches' Pyramid adds ways to integrate your personal Elements with your actions in the world. The insights provided by contemplating the powers of the Witches' Pyramid as they are used in your daily life can help you to trust your process.

The Elements, and their work and lessons, exist on lower and higher planes. The shape of a pyramid implies the planes of existence and the need to accomplish the work of each plane to rise. The pyramid must be built course by course from the base upward.

The Witches' Pyramid, when the prerequisite work has been done, is also a guide to spiritual evolution on the road to becoming your divine self. In Crowley's later writings, the mastery of the powers of the sphinx becomes an essential part of becoming an adept. When the powers and the consciousness of the Four Elements within can be elevated, it becomes possible for personal Ether to join with personal Spirit. At the boundary where they meet, the Quintessence that is made of you forms what can be known as the holy guardian angel, your god-self, the you that is eternal.

The Elements' behavior and attributes are altered on each plane of existence. In a sense, each plane has its own version of the Witches' Pyramid. When you rise high enough, their interactions become more focused on reuniting to become one. Beyond a certain level, the Elements cease to be unique and discrete.

> *Bless us, divine number, thou who generated gods and men! O holy, holy Tetraktys, thou that containest the root and source of the eternally flowing creation! For the divine number begins with the profound, pure unity until it comes to the holy four; then it begets the mother of all, the all-comprising, all-bounding, the first-born, the never-swerving, the never-tiring holy ten, the keyholder of all.*
>
> —a Pythagorean prayer

The tetraktys, sometimes known as the holy decad or the four lettered name, is an arrangement of ten dots in four rows in the shape of a triangle. It is a visual summation of many of the mystical teachings in Pythagoreanism from the 6th century BCE. It encodes their system of numerology, the construction of the cosmos, the Pythagorean musical scale, the Four Elements, and more. I have plotted the Elements, modalities, polarities, and unity onto the tetraktys, and it works well as a representation of the process of rising or descending on the planes of existence. This pattern is strongly resonant to that of the Witches' Pyramid and the cone of power.

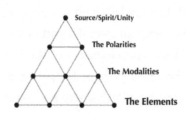

In my studies while meditating upon the tetraktys, I first made note of the many similarities between the cosmologies inherent in it and in the Hermetic Qabala. In particular, the flow from unified to differentiated through four states, four worlds or planes, and the ten dots that imply the spheres on the tree of life caught my attention. These thoughts led to the inclusion of the idea from the Qabala that there are trees within trees, and a recursive or fractal repetition of structures throughout the whole pattern.

With further research, I found that Dion Fortune and H. P. Blavatsky had also noted the same. Blavatsky wrote in *The Secret Doctrine:*

In occult and Pythagorean geometry the Tetrad is said to combine within itself all the materials from which Kosmos is produced. The Point or One, extends to a Line—the Two; a Line to a Superficies, Three; and the Superficies, Triad or Triangle, is converted into a Solid, the Tetrad or Four, by the point being placed over it. Kabalistically Kether, or Sephira, the Point, emanates Chochmah and Binah, which two, are the synonym of Mahat, in the Hindu Purânas, and this Triad, descending into matter, produces the Tetragrammaton, Tetraktys, as also the lower Tetrad.

Whether or not the teachings of the Pythagoreans entered into the stream that fed the Qabala is debated by scholars. Regardless, both the tetraktys and the Hermetic Qabala describe deeper truths in ways that are congruent with each other.

It occurred to me that the Witches' Pyramid might take other forms within the framework of the tree of life and the tetraktys. After some contemplation and experimentation, I settled on a form that I have been using since the mid-1990s. Tiphereth, the central sphere in the tree of life, is assigned the power to go and the Fifth Element as Ether, Spirit, and Quintessence. The four spheres that surround Tiphereth are the other four powers and form the base of the pyramid. In the diagram, I have added additional words for describing the four powers of the sphinx and the planets correlated to the spheres. To avoid confusion, I will refer to this form as the Greater Witches' Pyramid.

The sphere of Hod is assigned the power to know, reason, the Element of Air, and the planet Mercury. The sphere of Netzach is assigned the power to dare, desire, the Element of Water, and the planet Venus. The sphere of Geburah is assigned the power to will, the Element of Fire, and the planet Mars. The sphere of Chesed is assigned the power to keep silent, memory, the Element of Earth, and the planet Jupiter. The peak of this Witches' Pyramid in Tiphereth is also assigned the sun and the power of imagination.

Not everyone studies or works with the Hermetic Qabala, but even if that is the case, this form of the Witches' Pyramid can be used without that background. The construct of the five powers with an extended set of attributes works as a standalone, though any knowledge of the Qabala that you can bring to bear is helpful. There are some practical applications below.

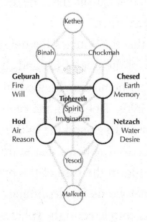

For the sake of clarity, here is a diagram of the tree of life with the placement of the Greater Witches' Pyramid indicated. Imagine that the sphere of Tiphereth is lifted upward to form the tip of the pyramid. There are a multitude of ways to assign the Elements to the spheres, worlds, paths, and pillars of the Hermetic Qabala. A close look at the various schemes for arranging the Elements on the Hermetic Qabala will show that they each display a truth that is but one facet of the jewel. The tree is multidimensional, and so are its various parts.

Please keep in mind that any diagram of the tree of life has less fidelity to the real tree than a flat Mercator projection map of the world has to a globe. These elemental assignments for the spheres work in the context of their use with this variant of the Witches' Pyramid.

Uses of the Greater Witches' Pyramid

This is just a sampling of the possibilities, but it should be enough to stimulate ideas on how you would make use of this construct. If you are using this as a part of a group ritual and have concerns about making the ritual too long or burdensome for attendees, you can set up the Greater Witches' Pyramid before the ritual. It is a durable construct, and it can function as a layer within or surrounding your ritual. When you are casting the Greater Witches' Pyramid, do not be concerned about having enough physical space to accommodate its shape. If you need to envision it as extending beyond your physical walls or ceiling, do so. This is a construct made of magick, not matter.

In casting this pyramid, it is better to include the names of the spheres, their planets, and so on, in addition to the powers. Ideally, use colors associated with these spheres rather than your normal correlations for the Elements. The color for Hod, the power of Air and reason, is orange. The color for Geburah, the power of Fire and will, is red. The color for Chesed, the power of Earth and memory, is blue. The color for Netzach, the power of Water and desire, is green.

A Powerful Warding

If you are planning a ritual or working that you believe will be prone to attracting unwholesome beings or to be buffeted by unbalanced energies, you may wish to use this pyramid. If you are creating the container, the sacred space, for the working by calling the Elements at the four directions, you have several options to choose from. One is to adjust your calls to match the arrangement of the Elements in the Greater Witches' Pyramid. There is no inherent direction when working with the spheres, so pick one and assign it a direction, then follow suit for the rest.

Another option is to create sacred space using your customary approach, then create the pyramid. If you believe the primary difficulties will be coming from outside the ritual space, create the pyramid so it surrounds your customary casting. If you are trying to keep things from spilling out of the ritual space, set up the pyramid within the boundary of your casting. The point of the pyramid should be seen as high over the center of your ritual space.

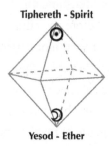

Tiphereth - Spirit

Yesod - Ether

If it is warranted, for greater protection you may cast the Greater Witches' Pyramid as an octahedron. Instead of calling the Fifth Elements as a unified point in the above, they are split into three. The point above becomes Tiphereth and Spirit; the point below becomes Yesod and Ether; and the space you stand in is Quintessence, which is between the worlds. If you are not conversant enough with the

Hermetic Qabala, use the sun and moon as your anchors in this casting.

To Focus Operative Magick

If the focus of a ritual or working is to produce results that are tangible in the physical world, it is operative magick. Some use the term low magick for that which produces material results, but it is an inadequate description that has implications about ritual style or value that aren't always true. This form of the Witches' Pyramid can be used to increase the coherence and focus of a ritual, spell, or working. Think of this pyramid as acting like a funnel or a lens that collects and concentrates the energy, information, and essence of a ritual to make the most of what has been raised.

The pyramid is cast above whatever the focal point for the ritual space may be. This may be over the center of the ritual space, the main altar, a ritualist, or whatever constitutes the place where the powers are to be shaped. The size of the pyramid may be only a bit smaller than the ritual space and be within it, or it can be just large enough to fit over the focal point of the working. Please note this pyramid is above you in the ritual space so that it can catch the powers as they rise. Direct your gaze and words upward as you are casting the pyramid. It is being created in an imaginal and magickal space, so do not worry about physical boundaries such as walls and ceilings when you do the work.

As the ritual builds, send the power into the pyramid. When the peak is reached, see the power become focused into a radiant star. Depending upon the goals of your working, you may launch the star outward to accomplish what is needed, or you may see the star descend into an object, a person, a spell construct, a servitor, or any other vessel for operative magick to empower it.

To Guide Timed Manifestation

If the timing or the location of what you are trying to accomplish is of critical importance, there is another construct that you may add. When you are creating a change that is to appear in physical time and space, there is a translation, a transition, from the way that time and location work in the other planes and how they do so on the physical plane. This shift in planes can sometimes cause your desired outcome to arrive too late or in the wrong place or form. To reduce the possibilities of things manifesting in less useful ways, you can create a construct using two pyramids.

The first pyramid that you cast is used as the method and container for creating sacred space. It is a Witches' Pyramid that is anchored to the Qabala but it is lower on the tree than the Greater Witches' Pyramid. Let's call this next one the Lesser Witches' Pyramid.

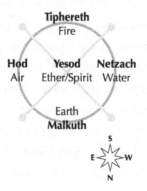

In this version, the Hod is Air, Tiphereth is Fire, Netzach is Water, Malkuth is Earth, and Yesod in the center is where Ether meets Spirit. If you look at the diagram, you'll note that this arrangement is reminiscent of the quartered circle that represents the sphere of Malkuth. The quartered circle of Malkuth is actually a visual summation of the whole tree. The first sphere above Malkuth is Yesod, so it is the center point that is elevated to form the pyramid. If you wish to add colors to your casting, they would be russet in the east, yellow ochre in the south, olive green in the west, muddy black in north, and violet for the above point.

The Greater Witches' Pyramid is cast above the ritual space as described previously. Once again, the Greater Witches' Pyramid acts to catch and to concentrate the power of the ritual. However, when the peak of the ritual is reached and the power has become a radiant star, instead of sending it forth, it is drawn down to the Yesod tip of the lower pyramid. It is drawn down by the power to go, by the power of imagination, by the power of that which is the triad of the Fifth Elements within you. Depending upon your goals, you'll draw it all the way down to release it either in our world or into an object or person.

Elevation of Consciousness

The Greater Witches' Pyramid may also be used as a way to rise on the planes of being to bring more of your parts of self into alignment. It can be used as part of a more far-reaching ritual or as a private working for one. Like all the things I've shared here, adapt it to match your needs and path. These are the essential steps:

1. Awaken the Elements and the powers of the sphinx within yourself. Do these one by one, following whatever order suits you.

2. If you will feel more comfortable, scribe a line of energy around your working space to create a boundary. Then, build the Greater Witches' Pyramid above you.

3. Find the place that is the center of conscious within yourself. Then bring the Elements and the powers of the sphinx into your center. Become a radiant star and rise up through your body and out the crown of your head.

4. When you can feel the bottom boundary of the pyramid, draw in the version of the powers that exists at that plane. As you feel yourself getting closer to the Tiphereth point, become aware of the star, Spirit, that awaits there.

5. Rise further up until your star of Ether merges with the star of Spirit. Take time to fully feel this. Then descend back into your body, endeavoring to retain all that you can.

6. Dismiss and dissolve the pyramid and any boundary that you may have created. Ground and center yourself and switch over to your normal mode of consciousness. Take notes of your impressions.

Closing

This chapter is a collection of seeds, of ideas to explore and applications to test for the various forms of the Witches' Pyramid. Contemplate the four powers, then add the fifth. There are many more uses than the ones touched upon here.

Think on how you do magick and brainstorm how you would incorporate or adapt the Witches' Pyramid to be compatible with what you do. Consider ways in which this construct can be added to other rituals or workings. As a prompt for your brainstorming, how would you use the Witches' Pyramid as a part of a banishing? I have done this, and it was quite effective. After you have pondered this for a bit, go to my website, as I have an outline for the banishing there.

19

Elements in the Landscape

Here, as we approach the end of this book, I ask you to go to the beginnings of human interactions with the Elements. The landscapes that your ancestors lived on and traveled through over countless generations and numerous continents and climes were the first dialogue between humans and the Elements. That dialogue continues today, and you have a part in it if you choose. There is quite a lot of study and practice with the Elements that can take place in your room and in your mind. Nonetheless, there are some things that are best learned and accomplished in the natural world.

It is a wonderous thing if you have the means and opportunity to venture out into the country or the wilderness. There are also wonders to be found wherever you can see the sky, the waters, or the land. The view from your window or apartment balcony is still a place to meet the sky. A river, lake, or sea remains itself when viewed from a bridge or pier. Even surrounded by tall buildings, you can still find the shape and conformation of the land if you look with eyes that believe you can. What matters is that you immerse yourself in the places you inhabit and see yourself within that landscape.

Regular exposure to the vastness of the sky, the sea, and the land is also a remedy for a human spiritual difficulty. When you sit too long, when you move less, day by day the body contracts and stiffens, and flexibility and range of motion diminish. When the version of the Elements that you experience is mostly an abstraction or fits in your living space, it is easy to mentally contract and lose your flexibility to know them in the vastness that is their truth. Even if your imagination is good and your psychic senses are sharp, it generally is not enough. Being outside and seeing the world as the Elements helps to remind you of that truth. I also find it inspiring and corrective to look up images from the Hubble space telescope and similar sources to contemplate the expanse beyond the sky that I can see with my eyes.

It may be that after reading these words, you've been persuaded to increase the quantity and the quality of the time you spend in nature. The probability of it becoming something that you do often enough to make a difference can be increased. Plan little or large outings and put them on your calendar or to-do list. Do an assessment of what you do on a monthly basis; find opportunities in your existing activities that would give you quality time with the Elements in the landscape, or see if you can easily add some.

The emphasis is on quality time not the quantity of time. The ten minutes that you take during your lunch break to really focus on some aspect of the landscape is worth hours of time outdoors without a focused attention. Although you may have good reasons for making pilgrimages to places of great grandeur, repeated visits within the landscape where you live will give you a deeper understanding. Additionally, being in the landscape where you live gives you an opportunity to see elementals in natural environments. The appearances and behaviors of elementals are not the same in formal ritual spaces versus in the wild.

Spending time with the landscape also expands and refines your sense of time. On one end of the spectrum, you see the quick changes of water burbling in a river, clouds changing shape, smoke twisting, and dandelion fluff on the wind. There is the middle range of a cliff crumbling over decades, of sun heat and frost cracking stones, of the turning seasons, and such. There is a longer range during which canyons are carved, shorelines change, mountains rise as magma pushes upward, and caves grow palaces of stalagmites and stalactites. There is the even longer dance of continents and oceans shifting, rising, falling, and remaking the surface of the planet.

You will also refine your capacity to change your relationship with time so that the twenty-minute walk at lunch becomes two hours of rich experience. The Elements live within the full range of time, and that is a lesson that they can teach us.

One of the powers of Earth is silence. If you have the opportunity to spend time alone in nature, or with friends who can manage some silence, you will begin to feel the quiet, the deep stillness of Earth. This will help you to listen more fully to the world around you, including the beings who are not physical. It will also make it easier to hear deeply into your own mind, body, and spirit. When you allow yourself the silence of Earth, the sounds of Fire, Water, and Air will be all the clearer.

The elementals also remember the history of life on the planet. They remember us before we were human. The elementals have seen the comings and goings of every culture and civilization. Many of these cultures do not survive as even one name or one story in human knowledge, but the Elements in the places they dwelled do remember.

The elementals also view us from outside the human fads, fashions, philosophies, and agendas that change over time, clarifying or distorting our history in equal measure. The landscape of the Elements contains storytellers and historians that know us in ways that we cannot know ourselves. They are our elders and are unaffected by how we desire to see ourselves. Every mirror reflects differently, and theirs is a magick mirror that can show more of time and space than we have yet imagined.

Liminal Spaces

It is easier to perceive and to attract the attention of spirits in liminal spaces, places that are thresholds charged with the power of ambiguity and paradox. Liminal places are rich with the power of Quintessence, which assists in opening the way between. The best liminal spaces for working with the Elements have natural boundaries, but there are good ones that incorporate human-made boundaries as well. You may wish to keep a list in your journal, or book of lights and shadows, of the liminal places in nature that you frequent. The summaries of your experiences in these places will be useful in refining your work with the Elements.

The seashore is extraordinary, as it is a place where land, sky, and sea meet, but there is somewhere even more special. There is a place called the sacred acre that is the land that lies between the marks of the low tide and the marks of the high tide. It is the land that belongs to both the spirits of the sea and the spirits of the land. The sacred acre, like the tides, is always in flux as it moves along the seashores of the world. As it shifts, its shape and size changes. As it moves, it travels through all the times of day and night, through all the phases of the moon, and all the seasons of the sun. The sacred acre is the moving threshold, the crossroads that walks, the liminal place where many realms and realities meet.

There, you may call upon the elementals of Earth and Water with great ease. If you have the good fortune to be in a location where you may build a small bonfire on the sacred acre, then the elementals of Fire and Air will respond as well. Whether for learning, communication, or doing ritual work, there are very few places in nature that respond as readily.

Crossroads, whether they be fourfold or threefold, are well known as places of power. The paths or roads are generally made by people, but some are also made by animals such as deer. The superposition of the paths made by organic beings onto the landscape of the Elements creates a distinctive kind of liminality. This is a threshold between varying types of consciousness, timeframes, and planes of being.

The sight of a crossroads is also a symbolic trigger that brings the idea of travel and encountering travelers, which helps to set the right state of mind. At the crossroads, it is easier to contact and to communicate with spirits of any kind. If the crossroads is in the countryside rather than in a city, the contrast of the threshold is stronger and makes it more suited to working with elementals.

Liminal spaces can also follow the axis of the depths and the heights. One of the advantages of these sorts of liminal spaces is that they provide access to another way to travel the planes that is not fully reliant upon human energy. These are more resonant to the central column of the elementals than they are to the human equivalent.

The entrance to a cave—or, better yet, a few steps into the cave so that you can see outside and deeper inward—can act as a gateway to descend or rise up on the planes. There is a predilection for descending, but you can also rise using this chthonic gateway. The top of hills, buttes, mesas, monadnocks, and other topographic features that reach skyward are also thresholds. These liminal spaces, like cave entrances, also act as conduits between the above and below. They have a predilection for rising on the planes but can be used to descend into the roots of the earth, as well. When you are standing at the top of a hill, or something similar, there is also a flow of elemental energy that you can tap into to empower your work.

There are also places that feel powerful and filled with elemental presences that don't fall into easily described categories. I have found powerful thresholds, neither/nor spaces, that were marked by dramatic differences, like a verdant field bounded by bare stone or a green pond in an arid place. I have also found liminal places that were very mighty but visually unremarkable, such as a small clearing in the woods or a small tidal pool. Some landscapes are complex and are made of more than one kind of liminal space or crossroads. In time, it will become a habit to inspect every place you go for its hidden gates, paths, and residents. You can also develop your capacity to make use of the powers of place—to the point that they will feel as familiar as your own energy.

Nature Spirits and Spirits of Place

Elementals are not nature spirits, spirits of place, or some type of Fae. Furthermore, they are not genii loci, daimons, nature devas, landvættir, or other related beings. I know that for many people and for some purposes, that soft and blurry boundary between different classes of beings works well enough. I find it useful to maintain clear distinctions, because that helps me to navigate interactions with these beings.

To begin, it is better to say that all these beings are made of the Elements, just as we are. Elemental consciousness is woven together to make their awareness, as well. The Elements also make up the environments, the landscapes that the nature spirits and spirits of place inhabit.

Another important distinction is that nature spirits and spirits of place often are partly composed of organic life force or are intimately enmeshed with pranic forces. In the case of nature devas, they are general tutelary spirits who guide, govern, or are the spiritual nexus for particular plants, animals, expressions of Elements in nature, and so on. In some traditions, the devas are also the summation of the group soul/spirit for individual species.

Landvættir (land wights), genii loci, landscape angels, and the like tend to be the summations of various kinds of life and energies of a specified environment, which may be as small as a pond or as large as a bioregion, a mountain range, et cetera. Spirits of place tend to have a composite, or hive, mind. Some are ever wakeful, and others are emergent and only exist as a focused consciousness when they are needed or summoned.

The term "Fae" has become a catchall term for hundreds of species of beings made of subtle matter. They have their own cultures, histories, religions, and agendas. As individuals and species, they vary wildly, even more so than physical beings. They interact with several planes of being, all the spirits mentioned here, and practice their own forms of magick. They work with the Elements and exhibit elemental powers, which can lead some to confuse them with elementals. They are of nature, as are humans, but like us, they can make choices about how closely they live with nature or not. They do share with humans what I call the Greater Earth, which is all the nearby planes, energies, and living beings that are anchored to this planet.

In observing the nature spirits, spirits of place, and all those who occupy the Greater Earth, much can be learned and discerned about the Elements. Seeing how other beings of similar composition in a shared environment work the Elements can provide inspiration into novel ways of making magick. Observing and listening to them can offer guidance in your individual and our collective evolutions.

Finding the Rays in Nature

After you have spent time in nature doing the things described above, you can take your efforts to another level. You may read this section now and will get some value from it, but it will be a completely different experience once you've put in the needed time outdoors.

It is useful to have a system, a context, or a grid for studying and mastering the Elements in nature. The three rays when articulated by the Elements produce twelve basic powers, and they are listed in the diagram below. You've encountered these earlier in this book.

Elements & Rays	**Ray of Power**	**Ray of Love**	**Ray of Wisdom**
Fire	Electric Fire	Solar Fire	Needfire
Water	Water of Shaping	Water of Unity	Water of Memory
Air	Commanding Air	Air of Mutuality	Pure Mind
Earth	Law Manifest	Eternal Return	Myriad Forms

For this work, I recommend that you set aside pages in a journal or set up a document on your computer, phone, or tablet—or any method you wish to use to keep notes and records. The first assignment is to look at the natural world and try to find examples of each of these powers. Don't rush the process, and don't move on to the next step until you have more than one example for each of the twelve powers.

The next step is to observe each of the twelve again but with the added task of trying to see how that power stirs within you. As the opportunities arise, find these powers within just as you did for the Elements in a more generalized way. Continue doing this, and you will develop a feel for how they work as you observe them.

When it feels right, attempt to reach out and cooperate with the Elements in nature as they perform their tasks. Keep notes, summaries, doodles, and sketches so that you can think more fully and deeply on your experiments.

As you build up familiarity with these powers, attempt to call upon them on your own for your own purposes. At first, you may have better success out in nature; but once you know the feel and the pattern, you will be able to use them in any setting.

You may also wish to see how the twelve powers manifest themselves in human affairs or in human technology and infrastructure. Once again, take notes and think about each experience. The twelve powers based on the three rays are a useful set, but not the only possibility. You could do the same with the twelve signs of the zodiac as sub-Elements as the moon passes through each. It is all a matter of applying a systematic approach to creating opportunities, documenting experiences, and applying the powers.

The Special Role of Plants

Plants are the most visible and powerful manifestation of life on Earth. When we first begin to open our psychic perception to experience the life force of nature, it is their vitality that we sense the most strongly. If we include the microscopic plants in the oceans, we also find that plants account for the greatest amount of biomass on our planet. When it comes to incarnate life force, nothing is greater than the plants in terms of quantity and prevalence.

The "green ones" also are our elders, in many senses of the word. Plant life was the first to develop complex forms at the beginning of life on our planet, when the distance between organic and elemental forces was small. It is plants that created the atmosphere that we breathe and continue to maintain its balance. They became the *alchemistry* that allowed animal life to arise. Our life force was green long before it was red. There are some remarkable similarities in the dynamics of chlorophyll and hemoglobin. It is here that we have the source point of copper and iron becoming the metals of Venus and Mars.

Every animal alive today has an ancient plant as its ancestor. It is curious that when most people think of human evolution, they stop imagining what came before when they reach the limit of animal memory and animal forms. This memory barrier, in itself, reveals a mystery. When the mode of consciousness and cognition changes radically, it is hard for memories to move from one format to another. This is true whether it is for an individual or a species. The memories are not lost but become harder to access. Nonetheless the older format is the framework upon which the new modes and formats are built so access remains possible though more difficult. It was also the plants in the form of trees that were the first homes of those primates that held the first spark of what we call specifically human today.

If you eat, then you owe that meal to the good graces we call the plants. Yet we often undervalue green life of the Earth, because it is so common and because the shape of the green life's generosity is so vast that we easily fail to see its boundaries. You would do well to examine this great boon, using whatever doctrines you adhere to regarding karma, fate, wyrd, et cetera. Under the influence of a culture that teaches contradictory values about matter and spirit, we tend to undervalue the green life because it is so earthy. Yet if we think deeper, we find that plants already have a more profound connection to the Elements than all but the most spiritually advanced humans.

One of the most universal metaphors for Spirit and its emanations is light. Illumination, enlightenment, and the light of the heavens is the goal of many seekers. In evanescent dreams and in transcendent moments, we may dance in the light, filled with its glory, but we do not remain nor can we be sure of the when and where of our next experience.

Plants live on light. Think about that for a moment, then think about it again. With the rising of the sun, their awareness is filled with light and the magic of photosynthesis. They drink in the pure energy of fiery light and combine it with Earth, Air, and Water; thereby they convert the elemental forces to the organic forces of life. In effect, they are like the Element of Spirit; the plants take the role of the center that synthesizes.

In a certain way, they are acting as adepts of Tiphereth on the tree of life. It is through their service that life is made possible on Earth. In addition to making food from light, plants are responsible for moderating much of the world's weather. All of this shows that they are servants of the light and evolution in the truest sense.

Before going further, I need to clarify the relationship between elemental forces and organic forces. Everything is made of the Elements, but organic forces are mixed, modified, and/or throttled down versions of the Elements. This is more of an observation than an axiom, but it is valuable to think of pure elemental forces as behaving more like direct current, and organic forces as being more like alternating current.

When perceived through psychism, elemental forces tend to move in straight lines and slightly curving arcs, whereas organic forces tend to move in circles, spirals, and sweeping arcs. Elemental forces generally move with greater speed and raw power than organic forces. Another difference is that organic forces have a greater likelihood of becoming entangled and enmeshed with other forces and forms than purer elemental forces.

It is also important to note that when we speak of the Elements within the context of living animal beings such as ourselves, they are not purely elemental forces. They are stepped down versions that have acquired a wrapper or a container of the proper shape that makes them compatible with our subtle bodies. Pure elemental forces lack the grammar of the language of organic life and do not recognize it. This is one of the reasons that there are warnings in many systems of traditional and modern magick about the dangers of too prolonged or too direct a contact with the Elements in their purer expressions. It is one of the reasons that there are protocols for safely working with these energies.

Inherent in the nature of plants are the protocols and filters that can translate elemental force to organic force and back. Not only do plants bridge the caesura between the elemental forces and the organic forces, they also are bridges between heaven and Earth. It is no fluke or coincidence that trees hold a place of reverence in so many systems and traditions.

In my estimation, the single clearest guide to the universe is the collection of wisdom teachings called the tree of life, the Qabala. There is also a widespread motif in many cultures and time periods that describes a world tree that is either the universe itself or the means by which to rise or descend to different levels of the universe.

In the pagan community, the grounding and centering visualization of becoming a tree is ubiquitous. The gist of this visualization is the practice of extending one's energy downward, like roots delving, toward the fiery core of the Earth; then upward, like branches reaching, toward the brilliance of the sun—all while increasing awareness of one's central point of balance. This set of images then sponsors an appreciation of the circulation of currents that, among other things, traverses the lower, middle, and upper worlds.

In the end, this is more than just a metaphor; for the forests of the world, whether they be oaks, firs, palms, or bamboos, are truly the organelles by which the collective being that we call the living Earth maintains its elemental metabolism.

20

Conclusion

There are many ways to name it, describe it, and mark its coming, but there is a growing plurality of individuals and traditions that recognize that we are in the churning of a passage from one great age to another. With that transition, there will come great changes.

Although the Elements change at a pace so slow that the entire history of humanity is but a blink, our capacity to understand them does change. With that change in what can be perceived comes new opportunities. This is the time when new ideas, theories, methods, and protocols will come into being, be tested, and be refined. I urge you to take part in expanding the possibilities for the study of the Elements.

Try to be more aware of the interactions, communication, and relationships that you may have with elementals. With the changes that are occurring, it is now possible to understand things that the elementals have to convey that would have been impossible to grasp previously.

These are beings who are our neighbors in the Greater Earth that encompasses the physical Earth and the subtle environments that are part of one whole. When we forget their reality, individuality, and sovereignty, we weaken our connection with them and the powers that are a part of us. I am hopeful that in the next few decades, work with the elementals of the Fifth Element will become a well-developed practice.

If you have been keeping notes and journaling your experiences as you've read this book, I encourage you to reread them soon. Looking at your own journey through these ideas will give you the starting point for deepening what you have and paths for new explorations. You may also wish to review your outlines, notes, and recipes for rituals, spells, workings, incenses, remedies, et cetera and reconsider them in light of what you now know about the Elements. One of the tried-and-true methods to retain that which you have studied is to apply it. If you also apply it to your existing work and practices, it will encourage the integration of the new and the old.

There are a great many sacred sciences and magickal disciplines that make use of the Elements. In some of these, the Elements are at their core; in others, they are tangential or act as a backdrop. You may wish to pick one of the sacred sciences or magickal disciplines that you regularly use and see how a closer look of the role of the Elements might change how you understand and use them. My readings using astrology or tarot have changed as my work with the Elements has progressed.

If you have tools that represent the Four Elements, the conclusion of this book marks an excellent time to reconsecrate, energize, and reaffirm your connection to your tools. I have done so numerous times over the years. Sometimes, this has been to strengthen what was already present. Other times, it has been to lock in new growth and insights.

Working with physical objects that you associate with the Elements is helpful. If you engage in arts or crafts, consider things like sheaths, storage boxes, holsters, pouches, and so on for your ritual tools. Elemental banners and altar cloths are also a great way to strengthen your connection and understanding. Find ways to use your creativity to expand the lore of the Elements, and you will be rewarded—others may benefit as well.

I'll end with a blessing to all who read this book. May the Four Elements become the Fifth in you. May the cycle of birth, death, and rebirth turn with the proper tides of Ether, Spirit, and Quintessence. May the roads, the spires, and the depths of the many worlds be open to you. May the Elements cleanse and enliven you as you become your truest self.

Recommended Reading

Arroyo, Stephen *Astrology, Psychology, and the Four Elements: An Energy Approach to Astrology and Its Use in the Counseling Arts* ISBN-13: 978-0916360016

Cunningham, Scott *Earth, Air, Fire, & Water* ISBN-13: 978-0875421315

Cynova, Melissa *Tarot Elements: Five Readings to Reset Your Life* ISBN-13: 978-0738758404

d'Este, Sorita, and David Rankine *Practical Elemental Magick: Working the Magick of the Four Elements in the Western Mystery Tradition* ISBN-13: 978-1905297191

Fennelly, Robin *The Elemental Year: Aligning the Elements of Self* ISBN-13: 978-1300499633

Lipp, Deborah *The Way of Four: Create Elemental Balance in Your Life* ISBN-13: 978-0738705415

———*The Way of Four Spellbook: Working Magic with the Elements* ISBN-13: 978-0738708584

Meredith, Jane, and Gede Parma *Elements of Magic: Reclaiming Earth, Air, Fire, Water & Spirit* ISBN-13: 978-0738757148

O'Donohue, John *The Four Elements: Reflections on Nature* ISBN-13: 978-0307717603

Trakhtenberg, Izolda *Life Elements: Transform Your Life with Earth, Air, Fire and Water* ISBN-13: 978-0980229806

About the Author

Ivo Dominguez Jr. is a practitioner of a variety of esoteric disciplines. He has been active in Wicca and the Pagan community since 1978 and is a founding member and high priest of Keepers of the Holly Chalice, the first coven of the Assembly of the Sacred Wheel. He has taught at many gatherings, conferences, and venues across the United States and abroad. Visit him at *ivodominguezjr.com*.

To Our Readers